Don't devalue your Self-Worth

A Woman's Guide To
Self-Contentment & True Love

NATASHA ARNOLD
AUTHOR
CREATOR OF
BELLEMEETSGLAM.COM

Prentice Hall

Boston   Columbus Indianapolis New York San Francisco Upper Saddle River

Amsterdam Cape Town Dubai London Madrid Milan Munich Paris Montreal Toronto

Delhi Mexico City Sao Paulo Sydney Hong Kong Seoul Singapore Taipei Tokyo

Dedication

I ask for the indulgence of the women who may read this book for dedicating it to a close friend of mine who is a man. I have a serious reason for this: he is the best friend I have in the world. I have another reason too: this guy understands everything. If all these reasons are not enough, I will dedicate the book to the father of the woman who wrote this book, My dad! He has been a source of inspiration for me and I just want to let him know just how much I appreciate him.

Dedication:

My Dad— Ronald Isom SR.

My Beautiful mom Bobbie I love you very much and I am so thankful for the woman you are and the women you raised me to be you are truly one of my best friends and my backbone .

About the Author

Born in 1993, Natasha is the youngest of five children, three girls and two boys. Her mother, a graduate of University Of Texas, and her father, a graduate of Harvard, instilled in Natasha loves of writing, reading, and education at a young age. Growing up in Austin, Texas, Natasha could often be found in one of the local libraries or reading underneath the shade of a tree in her calm, affluent neighborhood. In spite of her demanding academic passions, she is also fond of the outdoors, always seeking out new activities that she can enjoy in the parks around her home.

Her blog, Belle Meets Glam has reached a respectable level of popularity, carving out a dedicated audience that reads a majority of all the posts. She started the blog as a way to collect her personal writings, but it has since grown into something larger than that, attracting the notice and accolades of other writers in the field. Her style has been described as concise yet elegant, and her subject matter is often subtly connected to her own past experiences.

Her other interests include beauty, fashion, and home décor, all of which she considers to be an offshoot of her artistic side. She finds pleasure in interpreting works from the past and also in applying combinations of styles to her own works. She is an avid reader of Vogue, taking inspiration from the juxtaposition of various designers' lines.

Above everything, she aspires to master the art of happiness, staying on a path of constant progression and spending time with her family, whom she loves above all else. She is close with all of her siblings and her parents, taking outings with all of them whenever possible. As often as she can, she eats food at STK, a pastime that she shares with acquaintances both new and old.

Natasha considers her passion for writing to be life-long, something that she can continue to immerse herself in for many years to come. Her eventual goal is to settle down in New York Or Los Angeles where she can write full time and pour her heart into creating her masterpiece.

Brief Contents

CONTENTS

Preface

The perpetuation of the female anatomy is perhaps the most complex of the two sexes and due to this anomaly; it is not surprising that the sexual union between a man and a woman must be attended by an experience that is both sensuous and pleasurable. In recent times, females have been selected as the unreadable species and labelled with the preoccupation of sex and reproduction with heavy indulgence in love and self-sacrifice. Through longitudinal studies, experience and experiment, we have come to realize that the cognitive processes of a woman is not as complex as we first thought. A woman needs love care and affection though sometime exaggerated; women require a significant level of attention and care. Women are now awakening to the fact that the ideal expression of love is not just through sexual intercourse but through the lifelong commitment of a man to a relationship, attending to their every need and tackling the challenges as they come.

As the vast nature of our society expand even further, life becomes more harried and complex for the average female. Most females today find themselves living in a world that is immensely socialized, cultural and economized. These changes have made inroads into and encroached upon the very units that make up our society. Divorces have reached staggering proportions. Moreover, sexual incompatibly ranks high among the many causes attributed to this disintegration of marriages. The loss of the capacity for enjoyment and marital relations has become so common a complaint that it appear as if sex has lost its true purpose and meaning. It would also seem as though much of society's moral codes need reaffirmation and re-amplification to keep abreast of the complexities and to ease tension of present day living for single ladies young and old who are either in a relationship, getting out of a relationship or intended on getting into a relationship in the near future.

The author, with an empathetic approach, has set the task of bringing to the avid readers, enlightenment to the matter of relationship planning and execution as well as how to deal with a lack thereof. This authoritative little book represents the numerous researches and cross referencing of women from all walks of life who has a success formula to share as to how to get from being single to dating to being into a steady relationship and then to take the ultimate stance of getting married. The author then attempts to give proven strategies on how to strengthen the bonds of marriage as well as how to make this bond lasts forever.

Preface

Simply written and simply told, this book is a woman's guide to self-contentment and finding true love. It is geared at enlightening as well as providing a substitute to your own physician's advice. In past years, there have been so many taboos about single ladies and finding an alternative source of happiness, dating and the process of finding a mate and handling relationships from exclusivity to marriage and then some. Because of a continuous brain overload and confusing voices in their heads, many men and even many more women reach adulthood not only totally unprepared but actually troubled by fears, inhibitions and disillusionment about the fundamentals to be addressed when building and maintaining a stable relationship. Maddening, frustration, marked confusion and much unhappiness have resulted from a lock of knowledge.

In some respects, relationship directs our daily lives. To learn about building and maintaining a relationship and to understand its full nature is not impossible. The author of this book has ably presented the known facts. Courageous, honest and frank expositions are provided here, in clarifying specific aspects concerned with the human need for love and accompaniment, which is commendable. Perhaps for some couples who read this little opus, the ways of the female may be made more pleasant and clearer, and the impulses that bring them together will not be attended by fears, selfishness and or anguish. Romance, devotion, gratifying experiences and full-blossomed emotions will bind them. Knowledge and understanding will add dignity, honour and beauty to their most intimate functions.

This book by Natasha Arnold, partially completed with careful references from a wealth of other literature as well as from personal experiences, serves the purpose of enlightening the minds of woman from all walks of life, which is admirable and is indeed a real contribution to the understanding of planning, forming and maintaining strong bongs between married couples, encouraging the singles amongst us and training the present day daters.

Acknowledgements

The book Don't Devalue Your Self-Worth: A Woman's Guide to Self-Contentment & True Love, was an exciting undertaking and there are a number of people I must acknowledge for this awesome job:

I want to acknowledge how much I have learned from working with a few co-authors on more specialized relationship topics which aided me in successfully completing this book. I owe you all a great deal.

My overriding debt continues to be to my lovely family whom provided me with the time, support, and inspiration needed to prepare this book. It is truly a family book. I am continually grateful for the benefits I have been receiving from the wisdom of my co-workers and managers towards this book. I am also grateful in acknowledging my invaluable research and development help-team and their contributions to this book. A big thank you to all the faculty and colleagues from all the colleges and universities I collaborated with throughout the years in making this book a success. I owe you all a considerable debt.

I am also appreciative of all that I have learned from working with many Family Life and Marriage Executives who have generously shared their insights and experiences. With this, my first debut edition of this book, I received some extremely helpful research assistance from two former Princeton University graduates who were holders of MBAs in Social Psychology, they were as accurate, thorough, dependable, and cheerful as you could possibly imagine. My publishing house BMG ENTERPRISES provided me with superb administrative support as well, thanks to you too.

Finally, I give special thanks and commendations to God Himself, who made it all happen and made it all worthwhile

Don't Devalue Your Self-Worth

A Woman's Guide To
Self-Contentment & True Love

Objectives|

After Reading This Section, You Will Be Able
To Assess The Following

- Learning the mental processes of singleness
- Understanding how to deal with singleness
- Learning the factors that contributes to singleness
- Understanding the highs and lows of being single
- Maintaining composure despite your single status

CHAPTER 1:
Acknowledging Your Singleness

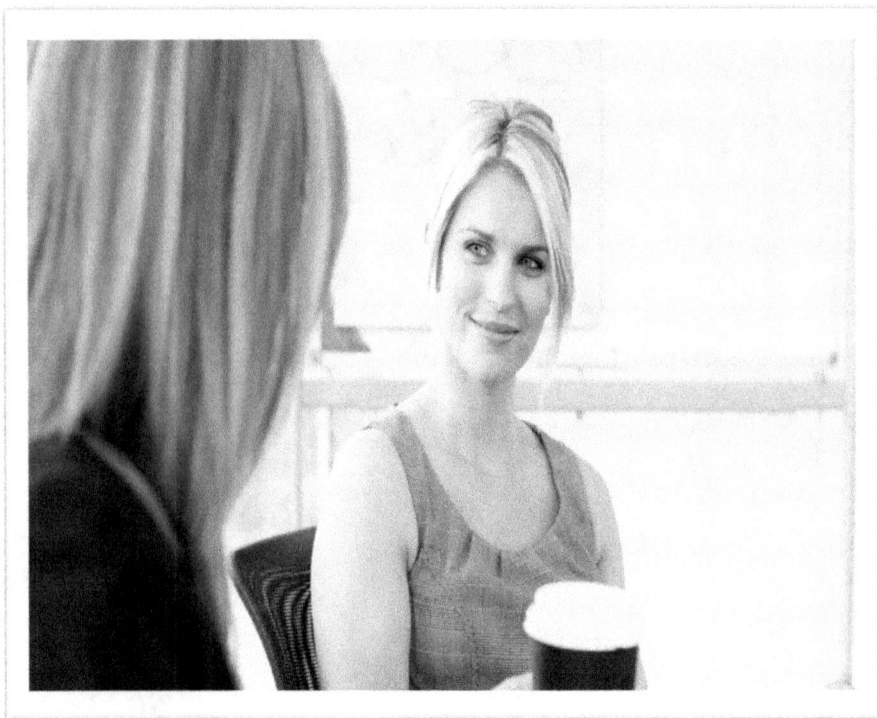

"You'll learn, as you get older, that rules are made to be broken. Be bold enough to live life on your terms, and never, ever apologize for it. Go against the grain, refuse to conform, take the road less travelled instead of the well-beaten path. Laugh in the face of adversity, and leap before you look. Dance as though EVERYBODY is watching. March to the beat of your own drummer. And stubbornly refuse to fit in."

—Mandy Hale

DENIAL

Pamela was in denial. She had dated Fred for 7 months and all was well until Pamela noticed that Fred had gotten distant and uncaring. He used to call her 5 times a day but that was now replaced with one call per night until the calls just stopped coming. She would call him but he would never pick up the call. By the time, he returned her phone call it was late at night and he would tell her that he was tired so he was going to bed. Pamela called Fred one day only to hear that his phone was no longer in use. Months passed and she still had not heard anything from him. Was he dead or alive, were they still in a relationship, or was she single again. Pamela struggled with these questions and she searched for answers.

Most people would have already gotten a clue in this situation but ever—so often, we as women live in complete denial of what is sitting right in front of us. We often try to justify why men behave the way they do in a relationships (Bettie, 2008). Men as well as women should be held accountable for their actions. The perception that it is a 'Man thing' should be irradiated from our thoughts as this gives way to selfish and immature behaviors that will only lead to heart break and hurt. We find that we are too easily caught up with emotional decadence to see the bigger picture and thus allowing ourselves to fall into diverse traps leaving us vulnerable and helpless in defending our honor as strong women. As women, we are to make known our expectations on how we expect a man to treat us (Ellison, 2003).

Let us not be naïve in believing that all men are the same or shares the same sentiment. Far from it, the warning signs are there, all we need do is take the time to see them and accept them. I'm sure Pamela, after months of not hearing from Fred knew in her heart that it was time for her to move on, but it was her denial that kept her trying to reach out to him. It was her denial that made her wrestle with questions that she could obviously answer herself but just didn't want to accept that Fred would do that to her (Redmond, 2008). In this case, rejection is a bitter pill to swallow and we have all had to swallow it at some point in our lives. It is how we choose to cope with these issues that will either break us or make us. In this chapter we will be exploring the essence of being single, how to cope with being single, understanding the does and don'ts of being single, living a fulfilled and happy life being single (Bettie, 2008).

THE SIGNS

A man's view on relationships and life in general are indeed different from that of a woman's, nor does he react to situations in the same way she does. Men and women see the world in different ways and often seek different goals in life. The first few months in a romantic, relationship is most often the pretentious stage where both parties try to show the best sides of them-selves (Uprety & Adhikary, 2008). Enormous efforts are made to portray them as being well kept and organized, even if that is far from the truth. What we need to realize is that even through this phase of a relationship, one can still see signs or red lights if not caught up with emotional charades of sweet words and suggestive gestures. The signs are there (Bettie, 2008).

It is always said that love is blind or someone was blinded by love. This is far from true as love isn't pretentious or deceiving. It is the individuals involve that chose not to see the real picture. They often fall prey to their own desires even though there is a red flag slapping them in the face. They get so entangled with playing this mind game of 'I'm so great' that less time is spent getting to know the person for who they really are (Holden, Froide, & Hannam, 2008). After this magical period has passed and the mind games have taken effect, both parties are now engaged in a meaningless competition of who is better than whom and thus the whole essence of truly getting to know each other is lost. By the time they find out where they have gone wrong, one party loses interest (the man), while the other tries to find ways to rectify what has already been damaged (the woman). The signs are there (Hobbs, 2008).

So, where do we go from here? Unfortunately nowhere... When a man begins to lose interest in a woman, he becomes distant, unresponsive, and sometimes rude. Some men are not great communicators and therefore it is easier for them to disappear than to confront the woman and say what's really on their minds. They use excuses such as work, being busy or being tired all the time for not being able to return a phone call or for missing date nights (Ellison, 2003). After all these signs, it shouldn't take you long to figure out that he's done and you will more likely be single again, which isn't the end of the world. It's just the beginning of something new that we as women must learn and strive to embrace in order for us to move forward in a positively illuminated way that will not only give closure but help give clarity in times of uncertainty. The signs are there (Bettie, 2008).

ACCEPTANCE

Accepting that you are single may be one of the hardest things a woman may face after a break up. They are so use to being in a relationship it seems like second nature for them not to be alone. They spend their days throwing a pity party for themselves and don't even stop to think that the break up could have been the best thing for them. Being in a relationship is a beautiful thing especially if both parties are genuinely in-love with each other. It is not a one-sided thing, there has to be a mutual understanding of what the relationship is about (Bettie, 2008). Therefore, when one party has stopped communicating (the man) and shows no interest in reconciliation, it is essential that the other party (the woman) analyze this situation, and after considering her options move on without hesitation, thus accepting what is (Bettie, 2008). This is very crucial in the process of healing and moving forward as this will aid in a better realization of the situation.

In most cases, acceptance of this situation takes time and it varies from individual to individual. It may take Pamela 6 months while it takes Kelly a year as well as it may take Davina a week. It all depends on the individual and their particular situation. Not all cases are the same and so, should not be treated the same way, different strokes for different folks. The same applies for men; after all, not all men are the same and shouldn't be treated that way. Men on the other hand, may take a shorter time to get over a break up just because they view relationship differently than women do (Bettie, 2008). Fate has always been a key opponent in our daily lives, while we plan for today, fate might have a different agenda come tomorrow. So, what should we do? There is no need to worry about the things we can't change but use wisely the things we can change. Unless we possess incomprehensible super powers; its best to accept what has happened and move forward (Bettie, 2008).

Easier said than done you say...Our mindsets have a great deal to do with how we perceive life. If we believe that we will never get over a break up, then most likely, we may not. If we believe that break ups are a normal part of life and that we are not the first and definitely won't be the last to experience a break up, then we will certainly move on from such phase. Yes, the mind a powerful thing, thus it is up to us to use our mind-set to take us to beautiful places. Our hearts will get broken and we will feel pain and hurt...but for how long? Our desire should not be for something that we cannot change but for something that we have control, which is our mind (Hobbs, 2008). It is eminent that we accept the 'what is' so that we will not stifle our emotional growth and therefore leave us stagnant in our ability to go above and beyond our expectations.

RECUPERATING

Now that we have accepted the *'what is'*, it's time to heal. The healing processes can be excruciating, as this is the time that is spent licking our wounds and trying to make sense of it all. We must not confuse recuperating with hosting a pity party. At this point, we must find solace in the reality this too will pass if we allow time to heal. At no point what so ever should we think that diving into a new and uncertain relationship is a part of the healing process. Many people use this opportunity to indulge their sorrows into new prospects that they themselves know they are not ready to take on (Hobbs, 2008). The very thought of being alone can be detrimentally scary for some people and so they absentmindedly grab that first person that comes along and make then smile or give them a shoulder to cry on. In order for the healing process to take effect, this idea must be shunned at all times. You must acknowledge that the recuperation process can also be the most vulnerable stage in acknowledging your singleness and therefore should be guarded with great alacrity (Hobbs, 2008).

We often find that at this point, depression, anxiety and stress is heightened leaving us at the mercy of anyone who wishes to come and take advantage of our misfortune. In cases such as this, we now need to get busy doing things that will build our self esteem and lift our spirits (Ellison, 2003). There are countless activities available that we can tap into to ensure we don't relapse and find ourselves back in a rut. This is the when we might need to spend time with a friend we might have neglected or get a pet. We now have control over what we want or what we don't want and this is an opportunity for us to regain our self-worth; focusing on what makes us happy. We now should place more value on ourselves, after all no one will value us like we will value ourselves. Taken an art class can bring peace of mind and bring out certain creative talents in us that we thought we never had. We should take this opportunity to get to know ourselves but to making us more inclined with our inner selves (Bettie, 2008).

This is a daily process involving patience and perseverance. There will be some days that are better than others in that you will feel as though you are not going forward (Bettie, 2008). You will wake up one morning and cry; which crying is a natural part of the process as well. There will also be mornings that you will get up feeling refreshed, confident, and ready to face the world with a brand-new attitude. The aim is to make sure every day that is spent in this process, is a positive step going forward; making sure that even with the tears, there is a sense of belonging and the self-worth (Holden, Froide, & Hannam, 2008). With each day, your motivation should increase as well as your will to make each day count for something worthwhile. Progression should not be tiresome but knowing that at the end of it all you would have conquered the demons of depression and failure. You would have learned a valuable lesson about yourself and your purpose in life. By now, you would have recognized your passion and the need to be in a healthy relationship that only brings joy to not just you but others around you.

CHAPTER 2:
Myths & Facts About Being Single

"If your attached friends are bugging you about being single (favourite accusation: "You're too picky!"), turn it around on them. "Do you know any gorgeous single men I could meet?" (This could backfire if they're keen to set you up and their idea of "gorgeous" is vastly different from yours. And it will be.) Alternatively, be super-sweet and tell them you're waiting for your ideal partner "just like you did". (It won't work if you snigger at this point.)"

—Rosie Blythe

THE MYTHS

For centuries, people have developed their own theories about being single and living a single life (Hobbs, 2008). There is almost nothing positive to be said about being single. Compared to the many stereotypes out there, being single is like a disease that no one wants to have and so our own misconceptions and anxiety prohibits us from truly enjoying the benefits of being single and living a fulfilled single life. Here are a few of the myths about being single (Hobbs, 2008).

- **Singleness means lonesomeness** – This is certainly not true. The only people who claim to be lonely are the ones who prefer to be lonely. It has more or less become a swear word in today's society. Single people of today will even go to the extent of lying about their social status in order to not seem like an outcast. They hide behind their fears of what others that are in relationships might say or think about them (Arp, 2014). Being single only means the lack of marriage or a dating partner; it's not a death sentence. Therefore, to call yourself lonely is unreasonable just because you lack one person in your life (Bettie, 2008).

- **A relationship will help you feel better about yourself** – First, you have to love yourself first. There are persons out there who are dying to be free from a unhappy relationship but simply can't walk away because of reasons beyond their control. If there is an issue with self, it will become worse once in a relationship because a relationship will not cover up or solve a problem. It starts with the individuals and their own mind-set (Bettie, 2008). A relationship is not an insurance policy for happiness and fulfilment, which must come from you. Part of being in a relationship is solving problems. If you can't solve problems on your own, you won't be able to do so with someone else (Hobbs, 2008).

- **If I'm single that means I'm a failure or something is wrong with me -** Once more, our mindset has a big impact on how we view ourselves. Yes, being single can be very disconcerting and certainly make people ask themselves "Is there something wrong with me?" Unbelievably, there is no one on the earth that is perfect. Our lack of confidence gives way to feeling like a failure and discontentment. Failing at something does not mean that you are a failure and should be welcomed as a lesson learnt rather than a cause for annoyance and ill belief (Redmond, 2008).

THE MYTHS CONT'D

- **Being Single is unacceptable** – Being in a committed relationship or even married is not the only life style. If you believe that being single is unacceptable, you will end up seeking relationships just because you want one and the sentiments that is to be had in a healthy relationship is lost and you are back at square one. What's unacceptable is that you're seeking to be in a relationship because 'it's the thing to do' or 'it's the in thing'. This kind of behaviour is selfish and diminishing, and will only end in further heartbreak (Hobbs, 2008).

- **Being single is a time to wait for the right person to come along** – This as far from true as north is from south. If we were to wait on the right person to come along while being single, some of us would remain single for a very long time or for the rest of our lives (Hobbs, 2008). Being single is a time to analyze one's self, to build a personal relationship with yourself in such a way that it will enhance the stability of your growth. The right person will come whether you are single or in a relationship. It is then up to you to make mature, intelligent decisions that will be of significant benefits to you in the future (Hobbs, 2008).

- **Being single is giving up or accepting Defeat** - Accepting singleness is not a defeat; it is rather a victory. Regardless of the way it sounds, singleness does not mean leaving the rest of your life to an unhappy fate of being single. Accepting singleness means that you have dominated your fears and anxieties about being single (Bettie, 2008). It shows that you do not believe the myths and stereotypes about being single. Accepting singleness means you can resist the constant feeling of needing to be a part of a couple, regardless of the influences around you (Arp, 2014). You are making the most of this time in your life instead of wasting time in unnecessary anguish. Most importantly, it means that you are content with who you are.

- **There are no advantages to being single** – There are many advantages to being single. For one, you are free to so whatever you want on your own time and in your own way without worry that it will offend your partner. You can live your life in such a way that it will be beneficial to you and your well-being (Holden, Froide, & Hannam, 2008). You would not have to deal with the technicalities of a relationship such as the fears, the doubts and most certainly not the arguments. There are many in abusive relationships that wish they were single to live their life however they choose but do not have a choice but to remain in such ordeal because of indescribable reasons (Hobbs, 2008).

THE MYTHS CONT'D

These impractical statements only serve to make the problem some have with being single worse. If you believe such statements, then you have possibly pursued relationships for the wrong reasons. Remember that you have to be happy with yourself first. However, it is difficult not to buy into these myths. The first step is to recognize the myths and realize they are not correct. Then we have the opportunity to resist them by being examples of happy singles (Hobbs, 2008). The way you feel about yourself is apparent to others, and if you seek a relationship hoping that the other person will somehow improve you, you will actually end up driving that person away. You have to be happy with yourself before you can expect to get along with others. If you believe that you cannot be happy on your own, you will be less confident and more dependent on others for your happiness (Ellison, 2003).

THE FACTS

As human beings, we have always wanted what we do not have instead of appreciating what we do have. We sit back and watch others in relationships and think, "Well, I should be in that too," we have almost never given thought about being grateful for what we have and making the best of our situation or status (Uprety & Adhikary, 2008). Do not get it twisted, it is wonderful to be in a happy, healthy relationship to have someone to share beautiful moments with and to enjoy the many other benefits of being in a relationship. However, there are also many perks to being single and loving your single life. The benefits of being single are endless and just as fulfilling as being in a relationship. Let's take a look at some of the facts about being single (Arp, 2014).

- **You can enjoy your own company** - If you can't stand to be alone by yourself, why would anyone else want to be with you? So many of us can't bare to spend 10 minutes alone with ourselves. We're on our cell phones, on online dating services, hanging out with friends, family, co-workers and basically anyone who will tolerate us until it's time to go to bed. Then, we can fall asleep and not think about the fact we are doing it alone. Spending alone time with yourself helps to build self-confidence and allows you to love and appreciate yourself even more (Hobbs, 2008).

- **You don't have to share your space with someone** – As a woman, having my own space is very crucial. It's a great feeling not having to come home and clean up after anyone but a pet if there is one or having to answer to anyone about how my day went or where I went (Hobbs, 2008). In my own space, I do whatever, be whoever, say whatever without offending anyone which may cause contention (Bettie, 2008).

- **You don't have to deal with his people** – We all at some point get tired of dealing with his friends and family. We try our best to make sure that his friends and family like us and so we pretend quite often to be someone that we're not. When you're single, you only deal with people you want in your life. You make it clear who is welcome in your space and who is not (Holden, Froide, & Hannam, 2008).

- **You can meet and enjoy all types of men** – When you are single, you have many options open to you. You have the freedom of getting to know different men and their backgrounds. There is no hard and fastened rule that ties you down to one specific person, unless that is what you want. I've learned to understand that all men are not alike, that most men are just like women—wanting love, connection and affection (Redmond, 2008).

THE FACTS CONT'D

- **You have more time to hang out with your friends!**- I love hanging out with my ladies, having girl talk, watching chick flicks, shopping, lunching, going to the spa and other things you can only do with women (Rosenfeld, 2012). We need a balance of feminine and masculine energy in our lives, and when one is missing, we yearn for it when we do not have it. There are a few married women that will say," I miss girls night out," but still haven't or can't join us because of the responsibilities they have to their spouses and marriages (Redmond, 2008).

- **You're not financially tied to someone** - I love spending my money the way I want to spend my money. I've worked very hard for it and do feel I should do whatever I please with it. If I want to do a spa day, I do it. If I want a new outfit, I buy it. If I want to blow it all in makeup, I blow it (Redmond, 2008). That's not to say that you should be financially irresponsible, but it's nice to be able to spend money on a nice dining room table or a trip to Vegas, rather than a vibrating man chair. (All right, the vibrating man chair has some positive qualities, but you get the point.)

- **You have more time with your family** – Sometimes being in a relationship can put a strain on the relationship you have with your family. You may have to move from the hometown you grew up in to be with the man you love and this sometimes put a dent in your relationship with your family (Bettie, 2008). When you're single and even if you live miles away from family, you can go visit whenever you want without having to plan months in advance (Hobbs, 2008).

- **You have time to work on you** - You have time to get over the past, let go of past dramas and traumas and say goodbye to those limiting beliefs about men and relationships. You have time to get counselling, coaching, group therapy, pray, chant, write in a journal or whatever else it takes to rid yourself of any remains of past relationships (Hobbs, 2008). Once that process is over and you have a clean canvas to work with, you can begin painting a new portrait for yourself in which you are being loved and loving someone back. You will notice that when you treat yourself well, men will too (Bettie, 2008).

- **You can create the life you love and want** – After you've had the time to work on yourself, you can now begin to create the kind life you love and want. You now have the handle to steer your life in the direction you want it to go without dictation from others (STRAUS, 2004). This is the time to make plans for the future or put into action any long-term goals you may have while staying true to the short term goals. You can finally take those cooking classes, sign up for ballroom dancing or enrol in that art class you've wanted to do for ages (Rosenfeld, 2012).

THE FACTS CONT'D

The Fact of the matter is that living a single life can be just as fulfilling as if you were in a relationship. Apart from the lack of intimacy, I personally believe that living a single life can reduce your stress levels immensely (Hobbs, 2008). The possibilities are endless when it comes on to being single, there is so much you can do on your own than if you were to be in a relationship. You are better able to facilitate your goals and what you desire in your life; you have more time to appreciate yourself more. You will also discover new capabilities that you didn't know you had and the only person that you will answer to is you. This is a time to rest assured that you won't be judgemental of you even if you make a mistake, you will be able to work on the weak areas in your life at your own time and at your own speed. It's all up to you (STRAUS, 2004).

CHAPTER 3:
Single...By Force or Choice

"With even the slightest upset, detachment soon followed. I didn't lose sleep over men, and I was too restless to be tied down. The grass didn't even have time to grow around my feet before I was planning my next escape – whether it was to another state or out of someone's life."

— M.B. Dallocchio

SINGLE BY CHOICE

Sarah and Gary have been in a relationship for four years. Their relationship grew immensely as Gary asked Sarah to move in with him. Sarah of course, said yes because she and Gary loved each other so much and she wanted to be with him just as much as he wanted to be with her, or so it seemed. For the first six months, everything was heavenly. They did everything together, Gary would bring home roses from work for Sarah and she would have dinner ready by the time he got home. Their relationship was in a good place and all that was left to do was for Gary to pop the question. As their relationship progressed, Sarah noticed a change in Gary's persona, at first she didn't think anything of it until she decided to ask him about the changes she has been noticing. To her astonishment, Gary became intensely upset with her to the point where he actually got physical with her.

Their arguments became more frequent and more severe as Sarah had to start wearing a lot of make up to cover up the bruises left by Gary's constant physical abuse. Occasionally she would go out with friends and they would notice her bruises even though she tried to conceal them (Uprety & Adhikary, 2008). She would lie to them about her bruises and before long, she was ditching out on spending time with them. She no longer went out with them on their normal Friday night 'girl's night out' jaunt. She stopped spending time with her family; she would only call her mother occasionally and pretended that all was well and that she and Gary was happy (Bettie, 2008). Sarah's self-esteem became depleted; she couldn't understand what went wrong; how could Gary just turn into an overnight nightmare, what had she done wrong to deserve this kind of treatment? (STRAUS, 2004).

Sarah tried to urge Gary to let them take counselling, but Gary refused, he said there was nothing wrong with him and if she wanted counselling, she should go by herself because she had the problem not him. Sarah was devastated. How did she get from being so happy and love to be so sad and dejected. She loved Gary with all her heart and wanted to marry and raise a family with him, but that was a dream that would probably never come through. Things between them continued to get worse. Gary even took up smoking and drinking and that made matters even more complicated. Sarah felt a sense of shame and embarrassment whenever someone would ask her about her relationship with Gary or if they would be getting married soon. Sarah knew in her heart that she could never marry Gary in his current state and she wanted out of the relationship. She finally made the decision to leave him. It was the hardest thing for her to do. Now she would have to rebuild her life without the intimacy and companionship she has had for four years and start life a fresh. Sarah was terrified of being alone, but she had to make a choice, she decided that she would rather be alone than being unhappy (Bettie, 2008).

SINGLE BY CHOICE CONT'D

Many of us have been trapped in abusive relationships for many years. We have grown so immune to the inhumane treatment of our spouses that we begin to think that it's the norm and that we are able to cope. We often make excuses for the behaviours of our mates because we would like to think that he will change but the truth of the matter is most of the time we are afraid of being single again (Ellison, 2003). Therefore, we turn the other cheek in anticipation for a change to occur, which may never happen. We sometimes examine the lives of our friends and their relationships and we believe that we would be better off in a relationship in order not to seem out of place or looked at as being a failure. There are tremendous amount of a women today that are so unhappy in their relationships but refuses to let go because of the stigma that has placed on them (US Stats, 2013).

Sarah held on as long as she could, and I'm sure it wasn't an easy task for her to walk away from a relationship of four years with a man that she loved but at the end of the day, she chose her happiness over what she thought people might say and think (Bettie, 2008). People will always give their opinion on what they think is going on in your relationship simply because they don't understand it and when people don't grasp the full idea of what is going on, they then start to speculate and with speculation, comes a whole other kettles of fishes hear says and so forth. No one knows best how we feel and what we feel except us, the person in the situation, who feels it, knows they always say. Why should we as women subject ourselves to such heart rending lifestyles, when we have so much options open to us in this era of increased knowledge? (Hobbs, 2008)

Like Sarah many of us hold on to stigma that if we are not in a relationship no matter how unhealthy it is, that we have given up or didn't try hard enough. In situations like these, there is so much a woman can do and in the end it is left to her to make a choice as to what she wants to do. It is unfair of society to stereo type being single as a crime or taboo or that once you're in a relationship, you will be fulfilled. Instead, they should be teaching that fulfilment comes from self-achievement and contentment. Love for self and respect for others should be taught as more valuable lessons other than driving the notion that only having a partner brings joy and fulfilment (Arp, 2014). If a woman isn't happy and contented with herself first, how is she to make a man happy and contented in a relationship? It begins with her and the choices she makes in determining her life's goal and aspirations which includes living a happy single life or choosing to stay in an abusive relationship where she might eventually lose her life (Hobbs, 2008).

SINGLE BY FORCE

Jenna was devastated at the news that her husband of 11 years only had 3 months to live. Kenny, Jenna's husband, had been diagnosed with prostate cancer and things weren't looking good. Jenna and Kenny were very in love; they did and shared everything together. For years, they have tried to have children but to no avail. Jenna and Kenny went to doctor after doctor only to be told that they were perfectly healthy and they should just continue to try. In the 11th year of their marriage, Kenny became ill with severe groin pains. Doctors ran tests and found out that Kenny had prostate cancer and it was too forgone and chemotherapy would be of no effect. The thought of losing Kenny was unfathomable for Jenna; she tried to be optimistic and to make sure she stood by him through every minute of his last hours alive. When she was alone, she would cry uncontrollably. For 11 years, she was with her soul mate and now he was leaving her for good. How would she cope without him?

Jenna had never been away from Kenny for more than a day much less for the rest of her life. Thoughts flooded through Jenna's head as she tried to figure out what would happen next after Kenny died. Her heart broke every time she thought about it; she could never go on living without her soul mate. How would she manage coming home to an empty house, how would she cope with the loneliness? All these thoughts and more filled Jenna's mind. Life would never be the same again without her precious Kenny by her side. Her family assured her that they would be there for her and soon she would find someone just as great as Kenny was. She refused to think there was any one that could take Kenny's place. He was her superhero and she wanted him and no one else.

As time passed, Kenny grew weaker and weaker and Jenna felt every pain he felt even though she tried to smile with him and comfort him. This was tearing her apart but she knew that the moment would come and she would have to let go. The day finally came while Jenna was sitting at Kenny's hospital bed as she held his hand in hers with tears streaming down her face. "Don't cry honey, I will always be with you and will make sure you're taken care of," Kenny said with a smile. This made Jenna cry even more, she couldn't bear to see him like that and to know that she wouldn't be around much longer. She listened to Kenny as he recited the vows that he told her on their wedding day, his voice grew weaker by the minute until there was silence. Jenny cried profusely as she hugged and kissed his face. As the doctors came in to pronounce him dead, Jenna held on to his hand in disbelief as she looked at him with compassion and love. Her only companion had left her and she feared being alone. Starting all over again was going to be tough and she wondered if she would ever be able to do it.

SINGLE BY FORCE CONT'D

Sometimes circumstances like this leave us bewildered and feeling alone. Many women like Jenna have to face the reality that their significant other has passed on and therefore forcing them to pick up the status of being single again. The feeling is in many instances, indescribable and if not careful will linger for years to come (Hobbs, 2008). The first year after a spouse dies is extremely difficult. It is a year filled with firsts - the first Christmas, birthday and anniversary - alone. Facing these events on your own can be quite overwhelming. However, this is the time we need the help of our families and friends the most. There are also support groups that can help you ease into the lifestyle of being single again and coping with the loss. This will be no easy task as this is unfamiliar territory especially if you have been married or have been with your spouse for many years (Bettie, 2008).

Some days are better than others. There are days when you will feel that you can do it and that you have gotten through the worse and then there are days when you will feel as though you can't go on and want to lock yourself away from the rest of the world. This feeling can be so overwhelming that if not controlled can cause severe depression and anxiety (Ellison, 2003). I've seen cases where women ended up in mental hospitals and psych wards because they were unable to cope with the loss of a spouse or being single again. It would seem as though they have lost touch with the outside world. That is why it will always be stressed that you find support groups and stay close to family in this critical time. Most women often feel that they can do this by themselves and tend to push family and friends away in a bid to take on the hurt and pain all alone. They get bewildered and depressed when the reality of them being alone or of the fact that they have lost a spouse, sets in (Hobbs, 2008).

While struggling with your emotions, you will often feel a sense of guilt because you feel like you could have done more to help your dyeing spouse (Bettie, 2008). These feelings are intense and haunting and sometimes gives way thoughts and of suicide. It is vital that you never stay alone during this time as your thoughts and emotions may not be stable. Surround yourself with close friends that will make you laugh and encourage you in this your time of grief (Hobbs, 2008). If you're affiliated with a religious organization, this could be a great time to exercise your faith in your belief as this can help in a tremendous way. Take heart in knowing that things will get better as time goes by; time heals and restores (Holden, Froide, & Hannam, 2008). Allow yourself ample time to get pass the hurt and pain that you might being feeling because of the loss of a spouse, there is no set time for this as it varies from individual to individual. Maybe this is the time to take that vacation that you guys have been wanting to take, knowing that it would have made your spouse happy to see you up and about enjoying yourself to the fullest, you deserve happiness, you deserve, serenity peace and tranquillity (Uprety & Adhikary, 2008).

CHAPTER 4:
Dos & Don'ts of Being Single

"It wasn't easy to understand how the love between two other people could diminish you. If those two people were still accessible to you, if they called you all the time, if they asked you to come into the city for the weekend as you'd always done, then why shouldn't you feel, suddenly, intensely lonely?"

— Meg Wolitzer

OKAY, SO I'M SINGLE...NOW WHAT!

Celeste has been single for just a little over a year now. It's been a difficult transition from being married for seven years; the divorce wasn't such a hassle because there were no children involved. However, Celeste had no idea that she would have a divorce status attached to her name or even worse being single. It all became so unreal at first, moving into a new apartment alone and trying to cope with the reality of being single again. She was not ready for the emotions that would embody her as she began this journey of being a single woman again. At this point, Celeste is as confused as a dream; she now has to reorganize her life to fit her current state of mind and lifestyle. Just like Celeste, some of us have been affected by this plight in some way or another and it is often difficult to get a stern footing on what to do and what not to do. Here are a few tips on the dos and don'ts of being single.

DON'T even think of hurting yourself – At this moment, your emotions are unstable and you may have thoughts of inflicting self-pain or even suicide. This will not help your situation at all. You will be causing family and friends much pain and heart ache if this course of action was to be taken. It is advised that if thoughts such as these should present themselves, you should seek help from support groups, relatives and friends (Redmond, 2008).

DO take this time to get to know you better – This is the time when you will be going out on a lot of dates with yourself. It's a time for relaxed walks on the beach or quiet strolls in the park (Redmond, 2008). If you aren't happy spending time with yourself or by yourself, how do you expect others to like spending time with you?

DON'T lock yourself away from the outside world – Yes, it will hurt, but it is no use locking yourself away from everyone that loves and cares for you. This will only make things worse as doing this will only result in unnecessary reminiscing of the past and will only cause more pain and heartache. It is best to have the company of a few good friends that will help in cushioning the experience at this critical moment (Ellison, 2003).

DO spend quality time with family and friends – Family and friend are very important at this stage. No matter what the situation, your family always has your back. Sometimes we get broadsided by our relationships that we barely get time to spend with our family and close friends (Arp, 2014). This is essential, as it will help to ease the atmosphere of loneliness.

DON'T spend your days drowning in your sorrows – Why torture yourself by getting up every day and crying over spilt milk. At this particular point in time, you are very fragile and therefore should be extremely careful how you spend your days (Bettie, 2008). It is best to spend this time channelling happy thoughts that will uplift your spirit and give you the courage to move one.

OKAY, SO I'M SINGLE...NOW WHAT! CONT'D

DO give yourself time to heal – Time heals all wounds. It varies from individuals and their specific needs but with time, your heart won't seem so fragile and torn any more. Once you have given yourself time to heal, it will be easier to go forward with a more positive outlook on life (Hobbs, 2008).

DON'T think that you're a failure because you're single – Where there is life there is hope. The only failure is if you decide to give up on life and no longer want to fight for your happiness. This time is not to be used as a pity part; it should be celebrated as a gift (Ellison, 2003).

DO take on activities that will help in building self- awareness and self-esteem – Being self-aware is know what you want, what motivates you, what your weaknesses and strengths are, how you relate to other and so much more. We often lose ourselves after a break up. We tend to use this nation as an opportunity to eat whatever we want, even if we know its unhealthy, we stop exercising and trying to live healthy. This is not an excuse to let yourself go, this is an opportunity to build your character whilst resisting the temptation of unhealthy foods and activities. Enrol yourself into an art class or that cooking class you've wanted to take for so long. They say the way to a man's heart is through his stomach (Bettie, 2008).

DON'T be an accessory to group dates – Going out on group dates is fine, but make sure you're not the odd one out or you're being a third wheeler. Seeing your friends peered up with partners and who are left to tag along isn't exactly helping you to stay positive and unperturbed (Hobbs, 2008).

DO be open to the prospects of dating again - Now that you're single, it is not the end of the world or the end of your life. You will still have urges and needs that need to be tended to. As humans, we were created to be social beings, it was not intended for any of us to be alone and therefore, we shouldn't feel the need to cut off all prospects in our lives that might yield greater more substantial opportunities. We should endeavour to be as open minded to the possibilities without seeming desperate or cheap (Arp, 2014).

DON'T label all men as being the same as your ex – categorizing all men to be the same is an ignorant perception of thought. Just because you had a bad experience with your ex doesn't mean that all men are the same and that you should treat them as such. The good shouldn't have to suffer for the bad and in most cases, sadly, that's the way it usually turn out (Redmond, 2008). This kind of thinking will only lead to ruin and you would have missed out on an opportunity to be happy but was too busy building up a cement wall to notice that there could be someone out there that could bring joy and happiness to your life if only you gave them a chance (Uprety & Adhikary, 2008).

SINGLE GIRLS CODE OF HONOUR

Single ladies should not live their lives on a sheet of paper term as a time table, throughout our process of development; we've learnt to craft goals and aspirations in a bid to shape our destiny. Aspirations helps us to shape others expectation of us as well as our expectation of ourselves. Though some expectation are good for us such as finding that one true guy that makes us weak in the knees, tying the knot, having a promising career and wonderful kids, all these are great expectations; however, some expectations often morph themselves into unreasonable criteria for womanhood that consequent starts haunting us if we don't achieve them in the order or time frame expected (Uprety & Adhikary, 2008). For instance, Julia is a 21 years old Latino whose family believes that she needs to get married by age 26 and be done with having her four kids by age 30 For example, saying "I need to be married by the time I'm 24 and be done having kids by 32. Setting such a complex regiment for young Julia can become extremely pressuring especially if she turns 23 and still haven't found the love of her life to get married by 24. This could become really challenging if by her 25 birthday she is still unable to find that mate, and anxiety starts taking hold on her, Julia may even start have feelings of low self-esteem and start rushing to find that guy above and beyond her limits no matter the cost before she turns 26. Feelings and inadequacy and despair take over and Julia even starts having suicidal thought as a result of her plight. Instead, we advise Julia to leave herself open to find truelove at any time you may still keep you expectation but just know that it's not a crime if they are not realized on time (Bettie, 2008). .

Single ladies should never wait for company to do what they want to do. Many single women put of travel plans or explorations packages just because they don't have anyone to do it with, here they may even put off taking a class or doing some something really fun because they would prefer doing it with a companion. Life is extremely too short to believing it based on the terms of someone whom you haven't even met (Hobbs, 2008). The advice here is to experience life at your own pace, experiencing things with close friends and your true mate can be enticing; however, giving up the opportunity to enjoy life in the present for an uncertain future in a bid to negate the awkward stares of others who may see you at a place where you should be accompanied by other and your alone is the same as pausing your life with the remote controller, it is ill-advised and should not be practiced (Bettie, 2008). Instead, live life at your own pace, throw away the security blanket and take charge of your future. Take a vocational flight to Hawaii, or do whatever else makes you feel happy and continuously placed on the "not yet list." Surprising enough, you might just find that you had the best time of your life, better than when you had company. You will have untapped latitude to put yourself out there that would be impossible if you had a companion. You may even be lucky enough to meet persons you wouldn't have met had you have company. Putting yourself in this position build courage and strength while providing a sense of fulfilment and heightened self-esteem (Holden, Froide, & Hannam, 2008).

SINGLE GIRLS CODE OF HONOUR CONT'D

Single girls should never allow themselves to think that there are no good men available anymore. Dating can be a frustration process for most single ladies, because approach it from the wrong angle and mind-set. The statement that dating is frustrating is never much further from the truth. Good men are still available, but they come in many different shapes sizes and appearances. Nonetheless, when a single woman indulge her time in finding true love and continuously meets and filters through myriad of sexual perverts, abusers and player, without finding that one true person that lift their spirit, you tend to write off all men as compare to all the others you had a bad relationship with (Ellison, 2003). Saying that all the good men are taken won't make you feel any better, actually it will make you feel even worst. You are left feeling discouraged and belittle. Instead, consider to work on loving yourself from the inside out and not the other way around following this same principle with the guys you meet. Good character cannot be easily discerned from outward appearance so look beneath the charms and glamour (Arp, 2014). Learn how to enjoy life as it appears now, in eventuality, when you find that special someone, he will add to your happiness rather than being the one responsible for it. Have an open mind; the love that you prescribed for yourself might not be the love you eventually end up with. Having a picture of your perfect mate should not distract you from having a chit chat with other guys who doesn't meet all the features you had in mind. The right thing to always remember is that every guy you date brings you one step closer to finding the perfect mate so stick to it (Hobbs, 2008).

Single ladies should refrain from sleeping around with random men. If you are providing the benefits of a fulltime commitment, why would he want to commit? The popular saying askes, Why buy the cow when you can get the milk for free. Don't allow yourself to be used as a disposable pleasure toy (Redmond, 2008). If you meet a guy who makes you smile in more ways than one, meets your core requirement, and you find that you are really into him and things seem to be going really fine, it doesn't means that you have to sleep with him to feel closer or insight exclusivity. I guy who is in it for the long hall will not rush to be in bed with you. If you force him into bed then he may just pull away even swifter than expected as he won't want to be exclusive with an easy chick (Arp, 2014). Here, he may be thinking that he got full pay for the little or no work at all. Most guys would love to think that they are the only man or one of the few men who had a chance to sleep with you, therefore if you offer him sexual favours before he even askes then he will be lured into thinking that this is one of your regular practice hence he will not want to commit to you. Instead, ensure to wait until you're sure that its more than just a crush and he loves you and wants more than just sex. If you really like him, wait until he shows you that he really loves you too. You need to allow him to work hard for your worth, hold out long enough till when you are certain all the fakes would have given up. If he still sticks around in the end then he's yours. Use this kind of perseverance and restraint before having first time sex with a mate (Bettie, 2008).

SINGLE GIRLS CODE OF HONOUR CONT'D

Single girls should not be pressured into proving that they are perfect and striving tirelessly to be perfect as no one is perfect. Few other self-induced pressures are as challenging as the quest to be classified as perfect. Though we know that the notion depicts that no man is perfect, single women strive ever so tirelessly to prove otherwise. Perfection is in the eyes of the beholder and not the behold they say so they spend their days trying to be perfect for the eyes of their detractors (Hobbs, 2008). This is interesting as this undertaking will more times than not lead to nothing but constant pain and heartache. Singleness does not mean you are lessor than anyone, so don't strive for perfection to prove that you are not inferior. Allow your detractors to see you for who you really are; if in your current state, they think you are imperfect then so be it (Uprety & Adhikary, 2008). Living your life trying to live up to the mark of a perfect woman will only break you further in the long run. Perfection is an unattainable and an irrational objective that is destined to reduce you to a stated of exhaustion and dissolution. Instead, you must work on your self-esteem refrain from the notion that you are not beautiful, intelligent, humorous, or rich enough, you need to stop proving yourself to others and start living life your way (Arp, 2014). Indulge in a session of introspection, consider perfection and what it really means to you and your drive to be perfect, then, ask yourself "What is there to lose if I don't attain this mark, what's the worst that can happen?" If the answer is nothing really then give up this futuristic pursuit.

Single girls should refrain from stalking their exes for reasons beyond natural understandings. Don't allow yourself to be drawn into stalking your ex's virtual and or physical presence (Ellison, 2003). Finding that you are constantly checking out his Facebook page for new posts and or pictures can be creepy and is a call for concern, we all are guilty of this sometime, some way or another. If you find yourself looking at his twitter account, Linkedin, Instagram account or any other form of account for his private information the advice is cease and desist (Holden, Froide, & Hannam, 2008). This form of behaviour never amounts to any positive result so be warned. The fact is you are only going to hurt yourself in the process, what's the best that can come of this? Say you search his accounts and you find no information to make you alarmed, so you are left thinking "was I that bad that he wanted to get away from me that badly and there wasn't even another woman in the mix?" Peradventure you find the picture of his kissing another woman recently on his account, you will then be left with the self-comparison syndrome where you try to compare and contrast yourself against his new found love (Redmond, 2008). Instead, bar yourself from accessing his information, if you are having problems desisting otherwise. Delete his number, unfriend him, unfollow him, and disconnect from his circles. This gives additional freedom to the transition from a hurtful relationship to singleness.

CHAPTER 5:

Being Comfortable In Your Single Skin

"Happily single, is recognizing that you are not in need or want of being rescued from your single life by a handsome prince because your life is pretty awesome, as is."

—By Mandy Hale

WHAT'S SO GREAT ABOUT BEING SINGLE

So you've been in a relationship for some years and now you happen to find yourself alone, you start getting panic attacks and having a nervous breakdown over something that isn't as bad as you make it seem. The truth is, you need this. Being single isn't a social standing, it's the state of being strong enough to live and enjoy life without depending on others. So, why is it so hard to find a level of comfort when you are single? Well, it's all up to you (Redmond, 2008). If you feel that you can never survive or be happy without being in a relationship, you probably will not be. It is all about the mind set you have. You have to want to be happy and content in your single skin. If you are going to depend on someone else to make you feel happy about yourself or to help you appreciate who you are, then you mostly likely will end up depressed and overwhelmed by being single. No one can build your happiness for you but you. It is okay to have fond memories about your ex or your past relationship but you have to draw the line somewhere, especially if is going to keep you in a pit for a long while. No one needs that. Your happiness is your main priority at this point and believe me when I say crying over spilt milk isn't worth your time or tears (Ellison, 2003). Start by holding yourself accountable for making sure that you are going to make most out of being single. The possibilities are endless (Bettie, 2008).

Is this possible, you ask. Most definitely! Being single is not a prison sentence and most definitely isn't lifetime of sorrow and distress as some may think. It is quite the opposite, of course there is that period where you've just broken up with your partner and there is that sense of loneliness and you feel as though the world is about to end. It's highly over exaggerated if you ask me (my personal view) but it is a phase we must go through in order to completely appreciate the value of being single and happy (Bettie, 2008). After going through nights of crying and being sorry for ourselves, it's now time to create that atmosphere of serenity and peace; a place where we do what we want, when we want, how we want. The ball is now in our court, it is now up to us to say what goes, who we want in our space and how we intend to go forward with our life. It's not rocket science, this is a time for us to find that balance we have wanted for so long but because we had been so engrossed with making that one man's happiness our main priority, we often times don't see that sometimes being single is more a blessing than a curse (Arp, 2014). For what it's worth, being single was one of the best things that could have ever happened to me. I was able to take better control over my life and what direction I want my life to go in, it's as simple as that. Use this time to make you a better person, to fulfil some goals you have been working hard to reach, this is the time to spread your wings and fly (Redmond, 2008).

WHAT'S SO GREAT ABOUT BEING SINGLE CONT'D

Don't get me wrong, you should definitely open up to the prospects of finding love again. You are not sentenced to being alone for the rest of your life, but take it in strides. Allow yourself time to heal and to get adjusted in your single skin before you decide to jump into another relationship that may leave you even more broken than the first one. No rebounds please! Take each day one step at a time, as second chance to finding true and well-deserved happiness (Hobbs, 2008). Find things you like to do on your own, like going rock climbing or pampering yourself for a day at the spa. You will see how much you have been missing when you finally get the chance to spend this time with yourself. You become comfortable with being single when it becomes normal. As talked about in the previous chapter, this process will vary depending on the individual and so the time it will take to get comfortable will be different depending on the person. You can start by making a list of what you want to do, the things you want to accomplish (Redmond, 2008). Set goals that you know you can achieve and even if they seem unachievable at that time, set them any. You may never know what fate has in store and you are able to meet these goals with little or no effort on your part. Being in a relationship should not be a necessity rather, it should b looked at as a bonus to your already enjoyable life. Be an extrovert, go out and enjoy the world, travel to places that you have always wanted to go and see how the other side of the world lives. You might just end up finding Mr. Right in the process and then you will be grateful that you enjoyed your single life so you can better enjoy having a partner (Hobbs, 2008).

Placing value on yourself means that you believe you are good enough all by yourself. Do not settle for mediocrity or relax your standards as some people might say, to please any one. It is okay to value someone's opinion but remember to value your own more. Never let other people's opinion of you get you down and out. People will always have an opinion of you whether you like it or not, it's just the way life is. At this point it is easier to please yourself that it is to live up to other people's expectations (Bettie, 2008). People will not always like you for you are and thus will criticize you because they don't understand you or mainly because they don't really know what's what going on in your life. This should make you stronger; it should help you to build your self-worth and self-esteem. Use this as an opportunity to excel, especially when they doubt your abilities do remarkable things without the help of a mate. As the saying goes "I can do badly all by myself" in this case, you can do great all by yourself and that's a fact. Being single can be so uplifting, learn to appreciate the silence. Get accustom to hearing the sound of your own heart; how beautiful it is to be able to live your life (Hobbs, 2008). There so many in relationships that are so overly indulged in making their partner happy or taking care of their man's well-being and making sure that his heart keep beating, they forget that their own heart needs as much care and affection as their giving to their partner (Redmond, 2008).

KEEPING IT REAL

Dana broke up with Ted three week ago. They were together for two good years until Dan found out about Ted's affair and broke it off. She made a choice to put her happiness first. But then, Dana came face to face with another problem. Dana felt like a failure and didn't want her family or friends to know that she had left Ted because of his unfaithfulness (Ellison, 2003). After their break up, Dana learned how Ted went around telling their friends how Dana was immature and selfish and that's why they had to call it quits. Of course they were all lies. Dana's reputation was scared before she could even tell the truth. This made her feel defeated and so she tried to stay away from her friends and that way if they asked any questions about the break-up she wouldn't have to explain herself or make herself seem like the failure they already think she is. Eventually Dana became tired of hiding out and decided to be honest with herself and her friends (Ellison, 2003). This wasn't an easy thing to do after Ted had already fabricated such a lie about the reason for their break up, who would believe her now. Coincidentally, Ted started dating Dana's childhood friend, talk about stab in the back. Ted cheated in her too even more than he did with Dana and then fabricated the same old lie. Everyone eventually saw Ted for who he truly was Dana was able to finally get the truth off her chest (Bettie, 2008).

Like Dana, we won't always feel the need defend ourselves about the reality of being single because we feel as though we have failed and could have tried harder to make the relationship work. We should not have to lie about being single or defend our reasons for being single. It really doesn't the way in which we became single or the reason for us being single, it only matters how we move on from acknowledging and being comfortable in our single skin (Arp, 2014). How will you move forward if you are in constant fear of being alone? How will you heal from your past relationship if you are not honest with yourself first and then others? The best thing to do is embrace being single and enjoys your life to the fullest with no regrets. Relax your mind not your standard. Don't let because you are afraid of being alone you run to the next man that shows some interest in you (Ellison, 2003). Way your options ask questions and live to please yourself first and then you will be able to better to please others once you are comfortable with yourself regardless of your social status. Never think for a minute that you were not good enough for the man you were with and that's why you are single today. Sometimes we get so caught up in being so superficial about ourselves we sometimes overlook that the problem wasn't about us but the man. Take comfort in knowing that no one is perfect and therefore the thought of you being too skinny or too fat or just not good enough goes both ways (Arp, 2014).

KEEPING IT REAL CONT'D

Get excited about being single instead of sulking and hiding. The time you take to throw a pity party, can be used to appreciate the many perks of being single. I know you must be saying, "Well, what about Valentine's Day?" What about it? It's nice to have someone give you a rose or a box of chocolate on that day but that's all there is, think of being single an opportunity to have many Valentines days with yourself. You don't have to wait on anyone to buy you a rose; you can get one for yourself. You don't have to suffer the thought of having a man and wondering if he is going to remember to buy you something nice on Valentine's Day (STRAUS, 2004). The only expectations you have to meet are yours and no one else'. Spend your time pampering yourself, laughing uncontrollably at funny "Paul Blart movies," play a funky jam and put your dancing shoes on, you must create your own happiness and don't just sit there waiting for someone to do it for you. According to Naomi Slivinski, a social psychologist at Oxford University, if we allow others to create our happiness, then we will be sad again once they exit our lives (Ellison, 2003). Slivinski is correct, we cannot allow others to dictate when we are happy or when we are sad, we can allow them to add to our happiness but not to create it. If we fall prey to this myopic thinking then we will forever be sad on Valentine's Day or any other holiday where we feel we shouldn't be alone. So take a chill pill, calm down, it's not the end of the world, you can have great clean single fun on Valentine's Day without the awkward morning after hangover when you find that he's gone without even leaving you a note (Uprety & Adhikary, 2008).

So it's New Year's Eve! You've been able to complete the year being single but suddenly the thought hit you that you had welcomed the previous new year with your past lover, suddenly your aura changes and you begin to sulk. "What's wrong with me?" You may ask nothing is wrong with you; it's only human to feel the need for warmth and comfort at such a time of the year, especially if the fireplace isn't warm enough. You must realize that you will be feeling this way long ahead of time and plan for it (Bettie, 2008). Being single doesn't mean boxing yourself into a corner and sulking, being single means that you are strong enough not to fall for every other guy you see but waiting until the time is right and the guy is right (Hobbs, 2008). Christmas is a season for bringing joy to people's life so get out of the house and volunteer to help someone, support a charity, feed some needy children or help out your mom with the Christmas dinner and spend the holiday with your family. Have fun with your siblings and play dodge ball with your dad. The New Year's Eve celebration can be a great outing for you if you spend it with family and good friends. Plan for these awkward moments and chart your way through them with much ease. In the end you will fee alive and strong. Only a few bored and gloomy people have the opportunity of finding true love, don't get trapped in that group. Breakout and be the character you hope to attract some day. To be a successful single, you must enjoy being single (Ellison, 2003). Work around the awkward moments as they come and enjoy your single status.

PART 2: Dating 101: Everything You Need to Know

Objectives|

After Reading This Section, You Will Be Able
To Assess The Following

- What to do on the first date
- Searching for the perfect match
- Signs of a genuine mate
- Going steady and committing
- When to quit it

CHAPTER 6:
Preparing for Dating, Am I Ready?

"Most professional women are always on the lookout for the best and the brightest life has to offer. We can't help but reflect back on our past dating experiences, as well as the ones we are currently exploring and those we've yet to discover. The best way to stay sane, we've found, is to know others are going through the same exact thing as you. This is where some very witty—and inspirational—dating tips come in handy."

—By Meghan Blalock

GETTING READY

I'm Janine Burton, a 23 year old Afro-American with no real skills at dating, but dating is something I've done, and actually done well. It's different from having a boyfriend or girlfriend; rather, it's the prelude, where you are given hands-on knowledge of the other person in the getting to know you phase. I've dated over 50 guys in the process of choosing the one true man who gave me all that I was searching for. To many, this would be a painstaking process but to me, getting to know that person I would spend the rest of my life with was crucial and worth the efforts. You may say 50 was just too much, but I wanted to find that one true guy who met my lists of expectations, which were many hence my sojourn. I'm now married with three wonderful kids and a husband that loves me, world-without-end and that's the reason why it was worth it. My advice is to keep searching, regardless of how deceitful and painstaking the process maybe, one day, you'll find Mr. Exclusive

Unlike Janine, most people often hit it off from the get-go, and the first time a future couple hangs out might be a laughing riot, culminating in a whisky-soaked conversation at 5 a.m. about their favorite bands. On the other end of the spectrum, one party might set their hair on fire half-way through the date. Nonetheless the purpose of this chapter is to prepare you for dating, equipping you with the skills to know when, where, how and whom to date with the least bit of hassle unlike Janine (Arp, 2014). The traditional dating community, which was once limited in terms of proximity, has now been widen due to wide-scale adoption of electronic processes since the dawn of the digital age, which we'll look at in more details in chapter 10. So how do we prepare for dating in this borderless world? The first thing to do is to understand what makes you tick. Seek out the flaws and the faults that you may have, and design a way how to work on your weaknesses (Arp, 2014).

Once you become acquainted with yourself then it will become much easier to see the virtues that would complement your personality hence you will desire for those virtues which are most closely in line with your preferences. You are now ready to do a profile listing of criteria and traits you hope to see in your ideal match (Epstein, 2007). Once this profile listing is reviewed and you feel comfortable with your criteria, then it's onto the process of choosing the best means of communicating mutual interests of getting to know him. Whether virtual or physical meeting places, the key is ensuring that all bases are covered, in terms of generality, safety and originality. If you have an outspoken, charismatic personality, then you'll meet potential dates everywhere: in line for the gas station cashier, at the yoga center, and even sky-diving (Arp, 2014).

CHOOSING THE VENUE

Most people rely on traditional methods of finding a date like getting friendly with a co-worker, visiting their next-door neighbor or asking their friends to introduce them to that hot brunette from last week's Christmas party. More young people are meeting through Internet dating by creating online dating profile, often characterized with an emphasis on serious, rather than casual, relationships (Arp, 2014). It is often helpful to remember that the people you meet online are basically blind dates, because of this anonymity; you may be at a greater disadvantage of being pranked. Try not to give out too much personal information about yourself online unless you are sure that they are confidential. For online dating success, follow the three golden rules: always spellcheck, post accurate information whilst maintaining anonymity, and finally, refrain from sending nude pictures to strangers on the Internet (FISMAN & IYENGAR, 2008).

So whether you go out or stay in, you should have fun doing it. That's actually the whole point of a dating. Dating can be classified as social events which allow you to go out (or sit in) and have some fun with the person whom you might want to spend the rest of your life with. For some reason, many people have surmised that a date is synonymous to dinner. Such myopic mindset results in boring dates! Females should allow for their date taking them on unconventional dates such as to the dog park where they can view the puppies on display. Take your date on a brewery tour to view the making of their favorite wine or liquor. You may also choose to rent a paddleboat and take him out to sea the sunset of the tropical sea, or you could browse in bookstores, get a vegan cupcake while watching a fire dancer (Bettie, 2008). Fight the urge to consume high levels of alcohols to alleviate the awkwardness of an unpleasant hangover. Indulge in activities that interests you, and your potential suitors will be forced to either bring their A-game or opt to do the things which interests *them most* on the second date (Hobbs, 2008).

Which sounds more enticing? Dinner and a movie, or, "Hey, do you want to get a gourmet turkey sandwich and then go bowling a few frames? I know this bowling alley that serves the best Tacos known to man. Then we could go what the sunset on the beach just a few chains away?" The bowling alley here really sounds more appealing than just a dinner and a movie. The more spontaneous your dates are, the more appealing they become and often speak volume of fruitful relationship. Always practice the ABCs of dating venues, Assess the options available, Bid on the ones chosen with your date (whenever you don't want to surprise him) and Choose the one that is mutually liked by both party (STRAUS, 2004).

SAFEGAURDING YOUR DATING EXPERIENCE

S O now you're out on a date with a complete stranger, but do you feel safe? A cool tip to consider when meeting someone new for the first time is to tell a friend where you're heading and how to get in touch with you, and maybe offer a soothing check-in phone call just for safe keeping (STRAUS, 2004). It is often said that most people believe they will be fine, especially if they are diligent in their filtering, but it never hurts to have a safety net. Blind dates can be the most devastating for some people as you are completely clueless as to what you should expect. Several abduction have been reported around the world duly referenced as a result of blind dating; So how do we safeguard this process. Simple, meet in clear, open, populated spaces, ask a friend or close relative to accompany you, and keep an emergency number on speed dial (preferably the nearest police station) in the event of any mishap (Hobbs, 2008).

Memorize the address of the closest help center and always travel with excess cash in case of any emergency. Women often date men only because they feel these men like them, and not necessarily because they like these men. Being liked is cool, but if you are not delighted for what the other person is bringing to your table, you're not obligated to date them. These are often the avenues men uses to abuse females sexually. Though there isn't an antidote for truly recognizing genuineness, the key here is to ensure that you are not the victim of unpretentious emotions (Bettie, 2008). These dates often lasts way into the wee hours of the morning and ends with sexual assault, abuse, rape or worst, tragedy. There's no crime in realizing that you're not clicking with someone whose is unconventionally disturbing in words and actions. Cut your losses, be the bad guy for a day or two, and refuse friendship from suspicious and corny men; this may just protect you from a whole host of ills (STRAUS, 2004).

You may have to go on dozens of dates, which may result in numerous persons having your contacts. That may then result in unsolicited stalking and constant trailing. Be vigilant and selective in the release of sensitive information such as phones numbers, personal emails or bank account information (Hobbs, 2008). Pay attention to details! There'll be variations in age, body type, income, parent and marital status, gender, sexuality, kinkiness, weight, height, location, and agenda. Follow your heart but think critically about the things you want and the things you do on your first and preliminary dates as these are the points where you are most vulnerable (Hobbs, 2008). You may discover a secret or weakness of your date if enough attention is placed on conducting preliminary background research. Maybe you are a non-smoker, and he is not or maybe he's a convict, seeking refuge at your expense. It's all part of your education but be very wise. One day, you'll be able to apply your expertise to finding the person you want to be with for the rest of your life (Hobbs, 2008).

LOOK FOR THE SIGNS

While our male counterparts can be of grave confusion for us as female daters, sometimes they can be the best when it comes to dishing out signs and clues to hold dare when deciding if they are in fact good boyfriend material. Now that you have access to this guide, you'll never be confused again (Bettie, 2008). Take a look at these clues:

He's a nice guy. Somewhere deep down you may hope that the Harley bad-boy is going to suddenly change — perhaps order you a refill when you head to the bathroom instead of flirting with the bartender. But really, he's just looking out for himself. A nice guy is just that: He cares about your feelings, is interested in spending time with you, and is courteous. This is hereditary, i.e. if this goes well, he'll pass it onto his son or daughter (STRAUS, 2004).

Being reliable isn't just something he saves for his bros. When he says he'll meet you at 7 p.m. he's there on time. And, after your third date when you left your keys in the cab that brought you home, he came over to sit with you outside your apartment until the locksmith came (FISMAN & IYENGAR, 2008).

He doesn't want to play games. He's not looking to just get laid, he's in this to find someone to date seriously. So, when you text him "I'm so tired today," he responds within minutes (not a day later) with a "Me too (Ellison, 2003). Want a foot massage?"

There's never a shortage of something new to talk about. It's only been four dates, but you already can't wait to tell him about your day and listen to him recount his.

You feel like you could introduce him to your friends tomorrow and they'd get along seamlessly. You don't have to worry if your friends will like him or make excuses for his behavior once they do (Arp, 2014).

He remembers the things you tell him. On your first date you told him your favorite movie was Ever After but you somehow lost your copy when you moved apartments. On date five he brings you a new one (Arp, 2014).

You feel comfortable around him. You don't need to pretend to be more or less of what you actually are. And while you're still shocked that he didn't make a run for it after seeing you in sweatpants, he actually seemed genuinely interested as you explained your sweatpants categorization: fancy, errands, sleep, cleaning, and sick (Arp, 2014).

AM I READY?

Wanting a relationship and being ready for one are two quite different things. Most people want to be happy with someone by their side who shares their life in a meaningful way but before that can happen there are certain things that need to be in place for a woman to be ready for that commitment (Bettie, 2008). Dating is the process of getting a woman ready for a relationship but how do we know when we are ready to date? Here are a few tips to help you:

She takes good care of herself—there is a lot of truth in the saying that you need to love yourself before you can love someone else and a good sign that a woman is ready for a relationship is that she takes good care of herself. This doesn't just mean physically, in the way she dresses and in her personal grooming (although they are both important), but also in how she treats herself (STRAUS, 2004). Someone who constantly puts themselves down or has difficulty accepting compliments or enjoying dates because they feel like they don't deserve it is unlikely to be ready to let love in even if that is what she desperately wants. Love is an inside job (Arp, 2014).

She wants a relationship rather than needs one—A woman is ready for a relationship when she is happy being single—she is not afraid of being on her own and is able to ask for help when she needs it—this is different from being fiercely independent and insisting on doing everything by herself. A woman who wants a relationship rather than needs one does so because she has so much good in her life she wants to share it. There will be no need for game playing because she won't be clinging to the relationship or trying to change you to make you fit the role she has assigned you (Arp, 2014).

She is comfortable in her own skin—A woman who is comfortable in her own skin will be present when she is with you—she will listen and take notice of what you are saying and not seem constantly distracted by her own thinking or critical of yours (Uprety & Adhikary, 2008). She will be able to sit comfortably in silence and won't fall apart if you have to change your plans at the last minute because she is flexible and has no need for rigid control over events. She will appear poised and confident and happy to talk about herself, life and plans for the future especially with regards to what she is looking for in an intimate relationship (FISMAN & IYENGAR, 2008). She will say what she likes and doesn't like and won't be afraid to tell you how she is feeling. When a woman is happy to be in her own skin it will be like she is holding the relationship in an open hand – happy to let it be without clinging.

CHAPTER 7:
The Do's & Don'ts of Successful Dating

"If you kiss on the first date and it's not right, then there will be no second date. Sometimes it's better to hold out and not kiss for a long time. I am a strong believer in kissing being very intimate, and the minute you kiss, the floodgates open for everything else..."

—By Jennifer Lopez

In the new millennium, finding someone to date isn't nearly as tricky as mastering the art of dating. Between online dating, singles events, and the old-fashioned in-person meet and greet, it's possible to date someone new on a regular basis. But how do you make the most of these chances to meet your perfect partner? How can you ensure that a first date, good or bad, is a learning experience rather than a missed opportunity? The following are the top three does and don'ts of dating don'ts:

DON'T: MISREPRESENT YOURSELF

While online dating is a valuable resource for the savvy single, there are people out there who misrepresent themselves. Don't be one of them. Just as your online dating profile should accurately represent who you really are, your in-person encounters should be equally authentic (Arp, 2014). Don't pretend to be something or someone you're not in an effort to impress a potential partner. You're fabulous just as you are and if somebody else can't see that, it's his loss. Besides, a relationship founded on lies and/or insincerities will quickly crumble. The common mistake that most women make is the projection of a character that is indistinctive of whom they really are. Not only will this spell trouble for the relationship as it develops but could also extend to future relationship via dynamic sculpting. Here, you acquire a tacit need to adjust your behaviour and lifestyle to match that of your potential mate. Not only is this painstakingly treacherous but it has serious ramifications for such a pretender. You may end up getting hurt or worst, being used for sexual favours. Even if you are lucky, the best case scenario is that your potential mate starts becomes distrustful and vigilant off your actions regardless of their nature (Arp, 2014).

It can become quite confusing when we view the common debates of what information or characteristics to share and the ones we shouldn't but it's not as complicated as some women makes it out to be. A rule of thumb is to gauge how detrimental the withholding of such a piece of information can be in the long run. If you think the information is extremely sensitive to share in the initial stages of your dating process, then make it known that you have sentimental issues that you would love to share with him whenever you feel comfortable to do so (FISMAN & IYENGAR, 2008). That way, you have a safety net to cushion the effect of appalling revelations, later in the relationship. Take care to not seem too secretive and enigmatic but rather, relatively opened yet slight obscured to wide-scale diffusion of personal information. Everybody has secretes that they hold dearly to their hearts and may even take to the grave, however, it must be carefully consider what we share two weeks into the dating process as apart from two years into the relationship. It cannot be overemphasized enough; that misrepresentations in terms of you correct gender, name, age and sexual orientation can result in dire consequences for both you and your potential mate. It is advised to tell the truth now as best as is possible, and get rejected now, than to optimize the other party's emotions and face dramatic disappointment in the future. Be wise and you will become the greatest first time dater in your neck of the woods (Hobbs, 2008).

DO: BE CLEAR AND REALISTIC ABOUT WHAT YOU WANT

The most successful daters are those who not only know exactly what they want, but are realistic about themselves and what they're looking for. Make a list of the qualities and traits you're looking for in your perfect partner. Then look at that list and ask yourself how realistic it is (STRAUS, 2004). For example, is finding someone who makes great money more important than finding someone who lives within his means? Or if you think you want to meet someone who's highly educated with multiple degrees, is that as important as finding someone with one degree but have had amazing lifetime experiences, which have helped to shape and educate him? Make your list, and as you continue dating, tweak it to make it as clear and realistic as possible. The key word her is continuous adjustment of your list. Do not include, things which are temporary and are likely to change in the next month are so, for instance, you don't need to itemize the skill of being able to play a guitar. This is not as important as been able to communicate with people from all walks of life. Some women are attracted to dark muscular men, while others dig slender lighter guys, though not entirely significant, appearances have always been a main determinant of women choices in partners (Hobbs, 2008). Some women hates the fat guy but love the athletic dude, she would never even give him a second of her time. These outward appearances though vital, must also be coupled with the innate traits that we can't correctly judge from just a simple glance. The point here is that women should not allow themselves to be drawn into the myopic thinking that all that glitters is gold. The inner self is so much powerful than the outer man (Arp, 2014).

Judging from the myriad of literature on dating, it can be concluded that we have be approaching it from the wrong perspective initially. Care should be taken in deciding the things that matters most. Most women expects to get a lot out of dating while inputting very little efforts in making the process fruitful. Regardless of your reason for dating, you should know that the sole purpose is getting to know him. The challenge lies where women often misinterpret the difference between dating and courting. The two terms are quite dissimilar and must be distinctly identified (Epstein, 2007). Dating is a process of scanning for the right match in terms of likes and preferences and life values mutuality. If we consider these definitions, then we would not be unwilling to date a guy just because he's a virgin. Courting on the other hand is more intimate and is often what a woman things about when a guy ask her out to dinner (Arp, 2014). It is quite fascinating how the average women view their potential partner based on material possessions like cars, houses and investments. The dating process has now been revamped and replaced by the courting process, thereby undermining the time which should have been spent getting to know the person on a general basis to now opting to know the person on an intimate level first before finding out the general things. The clincher her is that women should look at dating as a general social event and not as a personal and intimate process (Hobbs, 2008). Therefore it won't hurt to give the guy a chance to know you some more before you let him get into your pants!

DON'T: GET STUCK IN A RUT

Getting stuck in a dating rut or dry spell doesn't have to be part of the single woman's experience. Taking time away from the dating scene to breathe and reboot is one thing (and necessary every now and then). But getting stuck in a dating rut where you're either not meeting anyone or only meeting the same type of guy over and over again should be a thing of the past (Arp, 2014). The best way to avoid a dating rut is to get "out there" on a regular basis. And by "out there," I mean target-rich environments, at least once a week. What's a target-rich environment? It's any location where savvy and successful single men can be found in abundance. For the best results, choose a target-rich environment based on your own interests (Arp, 2014). Don't think sports bar (unless you're a diehard sports fan yourself), but instead think bookstore or singles event or museum fundraiser or political rally. Once you're in your target-rich environment, don't forget to smile and circulate! The onus is on to position yourself in such a way were the desired persons are attracted to your and the undesirable ones stay away. Dress to impress the appropriate mate, therefore, if you want to attract the classy type with a compelling interest on investments or probably real estates, then you must dress classy and at least seem to have interest in business or home ownership. Likewise, if you dress informally without care for modesty or nudity then you will attract those single men whose interest it is, to pick up random chicks for one-off relationship or discrete encounters (Arp, 2014).

The challenge is to know who you are and what type of men you're into and what type of men will be happy to go out with you. Once you can resolve this discrepancy then you are on your way to meeting the man of your dreams (Epstein, 2007). Often time, females overextend themselves in mammoth cognitive processes in a bid to grasp what they are doing wrong, because they just can't seem to find that one true formula to meet and wow that perfect mate. This however requires much patience and virtue as the process continues can become overwhelming but the end result is worth the efforts. If you find yourself in a rut where you keep on meeting the same guys over and over again, then it means that you still have some grounds to cover in shaping yourself into that desirable woman, suitable for your mate. Here's what to do when this happens, rehash the choices you've made that lead you to meeting these candidates, was there anything you could have done differently? If yes then make a note of this and try making better choices next time around. It may be your choice of amusement, your alcohol intake levels, your sentiments for the impoverished, your choice in food or even your choice in clothing, whatever it is, ensure make a note of it. Once you've made a note of this then you are on the route to correcting your defective dating life. There are two options available to you once you spot the defect, you either adjust to the preferences of your ideal partner or you lower your expectations and settle for someone within your current scope of mental decadence. Whichever option you choose, ensure that you are comfortable with yourself in the end (Bettie, 2008).

DO: LEARN YOUR RELATIONSHIP LESSONS

Instead of obsessing about past relationship failures, look at those experiences as valuable lessons. You can learn from any dating disaster, relationship gone awry, even a bad breakup. These experiences ultimately teach us about our own resilience, what we're really looking for in a perfect partner and how we can do better next time by applying our lessons learned. The dating process can be termed as a system of trial and error, where you assess how different personality types compliments or clashes with yours. The challenge here is the ability to analyse unsuccessful dating experiences and learn life lessons from them (Arp, 2014). Getting to that point where you can control the likelihood of success and failure in the dating process should be easy for the average extrovert, but this is easier said than done. The recommendation is that you seek guidance from a process known as retrospection. Here you will give careful thought as to your entire dating history, you must then identify particular pattern in the way these dating processes starts and ends. How similar or dissimilar are these encounters when the full summation and analysis of your dating history has been completed. In hindsight, you will more than likely see a clear pattern as to why and how each encounters started and ended, the challenge is for you to have an open mind and refrain from pointing fingers. Don't entirely blame yourself and don't entirely blame the other party, you must accept at least a reasonable amount of the fault for terminating the dating processes (Arp, 2014).

Whenever you terminate the dating process, give yourself some time to regroup and recoup. This time should be spent in complete introspect as you analyse the highs and lows of your progression. It is good to date more than one person at once so as to allow for platonic relations (STRAUS, 2004). Though some expert advise against the practice, group dating allow for a more casual approach to finding love and often times result in some of the most sensual relationships. So the suggestion is to change your approach and psyche as it relates to the dating process. If one-on-one dating doesn't work for you, then maybe you could consider speed dating as well as group dating. Which are good alternatives for those women constantly find themselves dating similar guys. Whether online or physical dating, the key to remember is to always pace yourself. Continuous improvements are critical in the pursuit of a lifelong partner and learning from mistakes will propel you to a superior state of mind and self-actualization (FISMAN & IYENGAR, 2008). Your safest bet is correcting your flaws (if any) and allowing yourself enough breathing room to feel comfortable and free with that one true person you feel most comfortable dating. Some women have drowned themselves in such sorrowful mornings that they fail to realize the genuine partner when they present themselves. Care should be taken to understand the state of mind that is desirable for dating. A sense of well-being, coupled with self-esteem often characterized an emotionally stable mind are the only combinations workable for such a process. Only such a mind-set can be expected to be successful in the dating process (Epstein, 2007).

NOW I'M OUT ON A DATE, WHAT SHOULD I DO?

The dating process takes careful planning and often requires a lot of practice before you can finally say you are a pro when it comes to dating men. Thankfully, with this book, as sought to simplify the dating process and make it more realistic to achieve success in such a fast pace environment (Arp, 2014). So now you're sitting face to face with your potential mate, what should you do to ensure that everything goes well? This book has provided, in no particular order, ten positives that you should embrace and adhere to when going out on the first date:

Do know enough about your date, so as to tailor the conversation to his background. Generic conversations are usually boring. Really study his profile to see what his interests are.

Do keep at least some of the conversation cheerful, funny and intriguing. If you haven't laughed at all during a date, things are going terribly wrong.

Do listen. Does it sound easy? It doesn't seem to be. So many people complain the other person never noticed what they said.

Do ask questions. The easiest way to show you're listening is to ask pertinent questions. Your date will be pleased, possibly even stunned and perhaps almost always impressed.

Do freshen up. Makeup should be a priority. Wear a sexy outfit that isn't too revealing or to concealing. If you're meeting after work, take your makeup, mouthwash and lip-glass with you when you leave your home in the morning and freshen up before you meet your date.

Do have ideas about what to do. Put some thought into this before you go out.

Do be on time. If you're always late, start out earlier than you think you'll need in order to be on time. You never get a second chance to make a first impression—and this will be the first impression.

Do make eye contact, but don't be weird about it. Talking to your date while you're looking around the room, texting on your phone or playing with your silverware is really annoying.

Do call the day of the date to reconfirm time and location. Call or e-mail the day after to thank them him a nice time. Whether the date was great or just an experience, there's no substitute for manners. It's the right way to treat people.

Do be warm, friendly and happy. It's all contagious, and it makes it much more likely you'll get the same reaction coming back to you.

NOW I'M OUT ON A DATE, WHAT SHOULDN'T I DO?

On the surface, dating may seem easy enough to most. However, there're plenty of ways to doom your chances if you are unable to recognize some of the detriments that could prove crucial for your first date. In these stressful times, it seems everyone has a short attention span (Epstein, 2007). Hence this book provides a comprehensive list of the things you need to avoid doing on the first date, in a bid to deter a total, dismal failure. In no particular order, these are ten critical issues we must address when we go out on a first date with a potential mate:

Don't leave your smart phone turned-on or worst, don't consistently reply to messages or run out to take calls. This interruption could work against you in a big way.

Don't talk about an ex. This conversation will probably come up much later when your relationship has blossomed. If you're angry about an ex, or are still pining for them, it will become obvious that you are not ready to move on.

Don't splash on too much cologne or perfume. Some people are allergic, while others just may find it too much.

Don't gossip about anyone. Trashing someone else alerts your date immediately that you have a mean or shallow streak.

Don't talk too long on the phone to your date initially. It could be fun, but it could also wear out your welcome. This is a really easy way to be misunderstood.

Don't bring presents until you have established a stable understanding of his likes and dislikes. Some men will feel too much pressure and move on. Others will stay for the wrong reasons.

Don't attempt to watch downer movies on the first date. The show might have great acting and a stirring message. But, if it depresses either or both of you, it can be contagious. It can not only make the evening hopeless, but the potential of a relationship, too.

Don't tell dirty, political or religious jokes until way later in the relationship. In fact, unless you are a professional comic, jokes might really be something to forget about until real love has consumed you both. It's too easy to offend someone you don't know well.

Don't ever be pressured or force anyone into having sex, not even a kiss. Carefully watch the other person's body language and if it isn't reflecting as being receptive, then stifle those urges.

Don't call immediately for a second date. Wait for him to make the first move. Likewise, don't refuse a date just to play "being hard to get". No one wants to feel manipulated or unimportant.

CHAPTER 8:
Tips That Works for Teenage Girls

"I like the bad-boy types. Generally the guy I'm attracted to is the guy in the club with all the tattoos and nail polish. He's usually the lead singer in a punk band and plays guitar. But my serious boyfriends are relatively clean-cut, nice guys. So it's strange."

—Megan Fox

TIPS FOR TEENAGE GIRLS

T eenage dating has adopted a new dynamical format that have shifted the very way and fashion in which teenage girls communicate their attraction and feelings towards the opposite sex. As it relates to teenage girls and dating, no questions, concerns or comment should ever be viewed as foolish, however careful thoughts should be given to each contention, applying key issues to applicable teenage girls (Arp, 2014). The question is often asked "How will I know the answer to all these questions, comments, concerns and queries that I have never needed to ask before? Dating tips for teenage girls are critical; especially in the predating season, as this is the point at which you are most vulnerable. This book provides a few of the major questions that must be addressed before you start dating. As already established in previous chapters, love can take you to great levels of highs as well as even greater levels of lows, the key is having a good guide to help you cope, this book has all that and so much more to offer. At this point, you may be having the strongest feeling for someone. However, if things don't work out between you and your new found 'crush' then this may be extremely shattering for you (STRAUS, 2004). Throughout this chapter, we will be discussing six dating tips to consider when matriculating from a teenage girl into womanhood. Firstly, we will begin with the tip of allowing your-self sufficient time to cope with the dating process (Hobbs, 2008).

DATING TIP 1: TAKE YOUR TIME

Most teenage girls are involved in dating while others don't. According to Dr Charles Wibbelsman, Chief of Adolescent Medicine at Kaiser Permanente in San Francisco, Most teenage girls feel the needs to have good self-esteem prior to dating. Dr Wibbelsman advises that teenage girls should only get involve in dating when they become familiar with themselves and know why they want to date and whom they want to date (Arp, 2014). Conversely, Dr Wibbelsman believes that you should make an informed decision and if you're not ready, he advises that you stay single until you are ready and hang out with close friends who are also single in a bid to ease peer pressure. The onus is on you to ensure that you are ready for all the mental processes involved in the dating. Bear in mind that there may be a procession of successes and failures; you must be prepared to deal with both outcomes as they present themselves. If you rush into dating, there is a 90% chance that you will fail on your first attempt (Arp, 2014). Know your emotional makeup, your likes and preferences and build a portfolio of yourself. You can brainstorm these attributes and jot them down on a sheet of paper. The next step is to match your attributes with a list of complimentary virtues. For instance, if you have a dominant personality, you may want to consider teeing-off with some having a warm and accommodating personality. Conversely, if you have a nonchalant persona, you may want to consider dating someone with an accommodating/dominant personality (Arp, 2014). The vast number of guides and literatures available has sought to close the gap between successful and unsuccessful teenage daters. However, a plethora of new issues and challenges have recently been discovered, that requires urgent attention and was previously overlooked by most of these literatures. Though this book is limited in terms of space, we hope provide adequate enough information to solve these challenges and close the gap in relations to teenage dating success and failure (Arp, 2014).

DATING TIP 2: FIND SOMEONE WHO LIKES YOU BACK

So you have completed a profile sheet of yourself and have also moved to cross-matching your personalities with complimentary virtues. You may now be asking yourself the question: How do I find that one true person who loves me back? Often times, teenage girls get emotionally unstable when the feeling they have towards their first crush isn't reciprocated. It may even leave you to ask question about yourself, "Did I do it right, did I choose the right complimentary virtues to lookout for, does this even work at all?" You may even start blaming yourself, "Maybe I did or say something wrong" The fact is that, there is no complete error free way of searching for that perfect match especially at this period in your life (Arp, 2014). The key is to always remember that love is more than a feeling. So if you just happen to feel like you fall in love with a guy you're seeing for the very first time, chances are, you are intoxicated by infatuation. This is not to denounce the possibility of love at first sight but the chances of this phenomenon happening are 9 to 1. The advice is to know that you can only, truly love someone after you have spent a substantial amount of time with them and become familiar with their way of life as well as their likes and dislikes. In a healthy relationship, the feelings are mutual. You can only get the reciprocation of love, that you deserve when you give it enough time to grow, says Steve Harvey, in his book Act Like a Man: Think Like a Woman. In a true dating relationship, respect is transcended from both parties; you accept, respect and have fun with each other. Consequently, if after you have analysed your current dating relationship, you found that the previous statement does not expressly describe your relationship, then there's absolutely nothing wrong with you. However you must not be daunted by this, rather, continue your search for this one true person that makes you feel loved (Arp, 2014).

We cannot stress enough, the importance of choosing your dates carefully. Most teenage girls often re-utter this distasteful phrase "I can't help who I fall in love with," this is so far from the truth. Undoubtedly, you do have a choice in whom you fall in love with and so you must act accordingly. You choose not to fall in love with the homeless man down the road, the pastor preaching in the pulpit or the policeman manning the traffic lights, all these are mentally controlled decisions that you had to make. In the same stead, having multiple options in the ideal dating partner to choose from, gives you absolute autonomy to choose whom you date and ultimately fall in love with and not the other way around. Think about what you are looking for in a boy (Arp, 2014). Are you willing to fall in love with just anyone? What causes you to fall in love? Is it a fear of being single, lonely and rejected or is it the result of peer pressure? All these questions must first be addressed before and absolute decision is made to continue with your fantasy of being in love. Love takes time to grow, and falling in love with some takes as much time it takes for you to learn how to read. You should never speedup the process or be rushed into this seemingly elite realm until you're absolutely sure that you are ready for the mental forces involved when being in love. Teenage girls also ask the question: "How do I know if I'm ready to date? All teenage girls develop at different pace and stages; therefore, if you find yourself being uncomfortable with the idea of dating, it means that you need more time to develop. Socializing with friends who are also single as you are, is a brilliant way of curbing you sense of being bored and alone. Teenage girls who start dating earlier than their mental and physical faculties will allow, often finds themselves been hurt and abuse at a tender age because they are unaware in regards to applying the brakes. Waiting until such time when you find the right guy who will listen and wait until such time when you're ready to say and do only what you want is your safest route (Arp, 2014).

DATING TIP 3: KNOW WHEN TO MOVE ON

Often times, most teenage girls will find it hard to admit that their current relationship isn't going anywhere or is at a dead-end. Instead the alternative is often taken where they give their all to the relationship and end up feeling excruciatingly devastated when things don't work-out as planned. The issue is that these teens often engage in life threatening acts in a bid to consolidate for their alleged misfortune. There are countless examples of people being scarred for life over preconceived relationship that has gone wrong (Arp, 2014). The advice is to approach relationships with express emphasis and generality, i.e. ensuring that you learn understand respect and adore the other party before falling for them, the onus is also on you to ensure that the other party respects, adores and honours you before you allow yourself to fall for him. The challenge we face is that teenage girls spare little time in getting to know their partner before falling for him. Here, the issue is to understand male dynamics, a male will be interested in you for a month or two if his sole intention is to get laid, if he wishes to have a fuller commitment then he will stay far beyond two months. Though this concept varies from male to male, the key is to read the apparent signs. Is he sincere in his dealings? How does he treats his mom and or other females, does he leave you to open the car door all by yourself? All these are telling signs to look for, if he can keep up this act for more than two months then he's a good actor or maybe, which is more than likely, he's genuine (Arp, 2014).

Control your emotions and don't just fall for the first guy who says he likes you. Par-adventure, you've fallen for his charms after the two months would have expired and then you found that he was a fake, he has turned mean and selfish after you gave him your heart. You must therefore know that this is still a game of trial and error where you win some and where you lose some. According to Danielle Greaves, Medical Practitioner at The Guidance Centre for Girls in Cambridge believes that when a boy refuses to give a girl what's she needs emotionally, she is at liberty to walk away (Arp, 2014). She believes that the hurt teenager will suffer by waking away now will be way less than staying the course and endure unmeasured torture. Take care in being sure you only date boys who have a clear head space. Ensure that they have certain values and morality that is highly accepted by the general society. Stay clear of smokers and drug users. You should only date boys who are serious about getting to know you (Arp, 2014). Hence, it is often discouraged to date guys who are a so-called hit with the girls; those guys who have so much other girls, just gravelling at their feet, that they can't even find much time to talk with you. This might seem like a no-brainer for many teenage girls but there are a lot of other girls who make the very same mistake and often end up being hurt. A guy who has one or more girlfriend is not entirely interested in you for all the right reasons. Especially if he doesn't treat you differently from all the other girls, be sure to notice the signs of a player from the early stages and don't get played into thinking that he loves you (Arp, 2014).

DATING TIP 4: WHY AM I ATTRACTED TO HIM?

Most teenage girl thinks of attraction solely on the basis of looks and personality. However, attraction also includes a person's aura (whether pheromones or the body scent that one becomes accustom to or even the scent of his aftershave or body mist) the way the individual interacts with you, both publicly and privately, as well as how they communicate with you nonverbally. Notwithstanding that sexual chemistry has a lot to play here, we have to understand that this is not an actual science and thus cannot be interpreted based on test and hypothesis. Studies have shown, although inconclusive, that pleasant warm and friendly people are considered as being more attractive than cold and distant people (Bettie, 2008). Sure, looks are important but attraction goes deeper than that, for instant, would you be attracted to a handsome, athletic guy who walks around your house at nights and bombard you with numerous phone calls in a bid to ensure that you weren't cheating on him? Most females would quickly get annoyed by this and immediately opt out of such a relationship however, this may not be as easy as you thought though. The challenge here is to understand why we become attracted to someone. Is it because he reminds you of a lost friend? Or is it because he meets the criteria of an idealistic mate that we have coined in the recesses of our imaginations? The efforts should be levied on understanding what it means to be attracted to someone, according to Miriam Webster's Online dictionary, attraction is the innate pull we feel for or to be close to someone or something, that is to say that we relish being in his presence (Arp, 2014).

Nothing is wrong with being attracted to someone, in fact it is recommended. However, care should be taken not to act on these emotions until you are well able to manage them completely. In the interim, get to know the person to whom you are attracted. Then make a clear, concise decision so as to ensure that your attraction is more than just a passing phase. Ensure that you're not just giving your trust away without merits (Arp, 2014). Trust should be earned and not freely bestowed on a newly found crush. Ample time should be given in an attempt to determine whether are not you can trust the person you are currently dating. Attraction only goes half-way, getting to know the other person is the key, to gaining and giving trust. If he is unknown to your friends and family, don't rush to trust him entirely, oftentimes your family can detect things that may be hidden from your love-struck heart. Trust is only earned when a person consistently displays their sincere virtue to you on all levels. He always do what he promise he would do, he never lies to you or other people around you, he acts the same way around you even when he is around others, he tries every woman including his mom with love and affection. All these are signs to show you that your attractions for him are real and not merely guided by looks and or appearances (Hobbs, 2008). Be vigilant, you get only one first date, make it count, have fun and give it your best shot. After all, you are learning from the best book on the market so stand secure.

DATING TIP 5: DISCUSS FACEBOOK BEFORE LOGING ON

Most social media platforms such as Facebook, allow for a clear a adversely pervasive way of presenting yourself to the world. Like many other communicative platform, social media has a tendency of highlighting the major benefits and major ills of dating online (Arp, 2014). Here all your flaws and all your complimentary attributes are on display for the world to see. The key is to be very concise and direct with the volume of information admitted to these social media. There have been countless reports of relationships gone wrong on social media, (Chris Brown & Rhianna, Mariah Carey & Nick Canon) which have left people feeling hurt and betrayed. This leads us to a very important juncture in our discourse; please be advised that in the initial stages of all relationship, it is often recommended that boundary lines are set and borders are erected. Therefore, if you are like a guy or he likes you and you both have decided to commence dating, it is always safe to ask him to refrain from things about you online without your approval. It is also expedient that you do not make electronic recordings of private sensual moments that should only be shared by you and that special someone, once created, it can never be safely deleted, no matter how savvy you are as an IT specialist (Arp, 2014). Items such as nude pictures and recording, text messages and private conversation on the cell phone should be kept as such, private! Any detour from these agreements should prove an immediate red flag from the vigilant and learnt dater. Bear in mind that sensitive information such as these, needs not be shared with the entire world and any deviation from these predefined standards should be seen as insensitive and uncanny (Arp, 2014).

The challenge teens' face on most occasions is deciding how to effectively use social media for their own betterment. The answer is quite simple. Define you scope using these media as your drivers of information. Find a niche or segment of your audience that needs inspiration. Use social media as an effective way of communicating to your desired audience, your goals and aspiration, then find creative ways of designing posts and blogs so as to boost popularity feeds of you network (Ellison, 2003). So instead of just using social media for personal gratification, you may want to consider using them to aid in the betterment of others within you spheres and levels. The major issue is deciding what to blog about, after this the task becomes a bit much easier. Ensure that you are comfortable with your social media status; this may even boosts your chances of meeting your perfect match online or offline. Take care to set privacy control on your accounts and accept friend request only from close friends are acquaintances, allow for value added activities such as fun tips and activities on your page (Arp, 2014). This will help to detour unsolicited viewers from you page. Determine the level of content you want to add on these pages and only add content of clean and authentic origins. Viewers often take things as they see it, therefore, if you want to be seen as a positive, no-nonsense character type, then you must provide contents and posts which mirrors such a character. Remember, social media by and enlarge is not bad, it the purposes for which they are use, qualifies or disqualifies them from being bad or good (Arp, 2014).

DATING TIP 6: DON'T DOWN-PLAY ACADEMIA FOR LOVE

Most teenage girls find themselves in an awkward position when it comes to dating guys who log behind in classes, they often engage in constant downplaying of their grades and scores just to suit the ego of their inadvertent boyfriends. The advice here is to be honest to yourself and to your boyfriend, if he can't accept you as being beautiful with brains, then he doesn't deserve your time. If he constantly takes offense to scoring higher than he does; you should probable seek a guy who doesn't take offense (Arp, 2014). Never compromise your academic aspirations for a guy who finds academic prowess offensive. The challenge is not even on academic here, it spans further than that, he may be gender bias and view academia as masculine in nature and so does not ravel in your joy as his own. Common mistake teenage girls make is to date guys that are more concerned about the brand of shoes they wear, rather than the college or university they'll attend after their senior years in high school (Arp, 2014). Don't allow yourself to fall into the trap of thinking that a less-smarter girl will make him happy. This is farthest from the truth. To test this, try to compete with him in other areas of his expertise, for instance, one-on-one basketball matchups. If you ever happen to beat him on any of the sets, he will surely be upset, even if he doesn't show it openly and or immediately. Surround yourself with the people who love you for the full person and or individual you are. Do not for any reason whatsoever, allow yourself to be undermined by the actions of your overzealous, envious, and dubious partner. If this becomes a major challenge, then the advice is that you look elsewhere for and ideal mate (STRAUS, 2004).

The notion is made for you to also watch yourself and pay attention to your own unequal thinking. You maybe mislead into thinking that he is envious of your grades; the only way to be sure is to ask. You should use his body language as well as his overall temperament to decide whether or not he is genuine in his responses (STRAUS, 2004). Know though, that you have absolute right to be seen as the strong smart, independent young and impressive young woman you assumed to be. The popular saying "If you can't handle the heat, get out of the kitchen" applies here (Arp, 2014). In the same stead though, be conscious of you aura and assess yourself to see that you are not too condescending in terms of boasting on your achievement. There are some lessons to be learnt from athletes and or sportsmen who showboats (Uprety & Adhikary, 2008). Be genuine in your self-appraisals and commendations. You may even offer a helping hand to him if will allow you to. Never allow yourself to be so consumed about what he thinks of you being superior to him is in terms of academics, that you extend less energy in achieving the best grade possible for your full efforts (STRAUS, 2004). If your mate can't handle you being smart and cute at the same time, then too bad for him. But never allow anyone to sell you short, likewise don't sell him short, and try to understand things from his point of view first. He might just be as attracted to your intelligence as you are to his strengths. In concluding this chapter, take great care in knowing the pros and cons of female dating, set a profiling of yourself and your ideal date, know when it is to move on and try a new make, take your time to search, understand why you are attracted to your potential mate, discuss social media aspirations with him and be honest about academia and never settle for less than your worth (Uprety & Adhikary, 2008).

CHAPTER 9:
Getting Serious

"Some think love can be measured by the amount of butterflies in their tummy. Others think love can be measured in bunches of flowers, or by using the words 'for ever.' But love can only truly be measured by actions. It can be a small thing, such as peeling an orange for a person you love because you know they don't like doing it."

— Marian Keyes

TRANSITIONING FROM A CASUAL DATING PROFILE

Most ladies have either experienced a serious relationship sometime in their lives before, either by accident or through voluntary actions. If by accident, it often occurs when we are fully into the other person whom we're dating which then matriculate into something more than the ordinary. If it occurs through voluntary actions, where we really like the person whom we're dating and it doesn't matriculate into anything much, then you'd probably be left wondering if there was anything you could have done differently (Bettie, 2008). To offer yourself a fighting just of being successful in dating, it is often recommend that you think back on your past relationships, determining what qualities made it obvious that it was now time to get serious with your date, as well as what things turns you off. Having a working knowledge of how you are perceived by others will give you a huge advantage in making it through casual dating and even to the stage of getting serious. Here, you need to understand how to handle struggles of transitioning from casual dating to a serious relationship. Here is a three-part guide to assist you transition from casual date to serious mate (Ellison, 2003).

BE INDEPENDENT

A few experts believe that you should label yourself as being unavailable even when you're not. Though there is some truth to the notion that making yourself seem readily available may put you in a flawed light of being overly desperate or unattractive, it is unwise and often ill advise to indulge in dating myopia or dating pranks. Whenever you feel the need to display an adverse front from what you truly are, it is often advised that you take a few minutes to think, and then ask yourself why you aren't having the fun and excitement you know you deserve to be having (Arp, 2014). Putting up a front and making yourself seem unavailable is sure to work well at the casual dating stage, however, how will you proceed once you have exhausted that stage? How long will you last before uncertainties, indigence, jealousy and insanity steps in? Alternatively, it is recommended that you act independently. Make cool and true relationships with yours friends and go out with them one or two times weekly (Hobbs, 2008). Take a trip to the gym. Indulge in the sport that interests you most. Practice playing an instrument, learn a new language, or take dancing lessons. The point is clear here; value yourself and your own time. Remember that a needy heart is a dying heart. Insecurity often pushes people to rush and enter into serious relationships in a bid to feel safe, and if wise, the other person can quickly surmise your intents (Arp, 2014).

SETTING BOUNDARIES

Women are often reluctant in setting boundaries for fear of rejection or worse lack of commitment. But the popular question is often asked, "Why would you want to buy the cow if you already have full access to the milk?" The same is true when we think of a causal relationship; why would a guy want to commit to you if you are already providing him with everything that he wants without the commitment?

TRANSITIONING FROM A CASUAL DATING PROFILE CONT'D

Finding yourself stuck in the in the stage of meeting an honest guy who is willing to move beyond the stage of casual dating, is often a warning signal that you are giving to much in the initial dating process (Anderson, 2013). Why overextend yourself to make someone else happy that you hardly know? Let the guy you're dating earn you innocence, compassion and love. For instance, if a guy brings you flower on the first date, this is a nice gesture but this doesn't say that he deserves a kiss, or even worst, sex. What if this guy ends up being a total jerk after he walks you home and you refuse to give in to his urges on the first date? Most women may be in constant marvel of what will become of their dating relations once giving in to the guy's inclinations (Anderson, 2013). Without a doubt, having sex too soon will surely scare guys away from making a full time commitment to you. They will use you only for their own satisfaction with considering how you feel. Holding off until you are sure he is the one is highly recommended, however you must know that, I guy who loses interest after having casual sex with you not only a douche-bag but also and idiot, the onus is therefore on you to reduce the hurt to be sustained from such perilous undertakings (Arp, 2014).

THIS HIDDEN PSYCHOLOGY BRAIN HACK

You may be sabotaging your own mind without even knowing, there is however, a way to determine whether or not you are a victim of your our inclinations. The next time you go out on a date, define the purpose of the date. If your date is to find the one, then that will be the main cause of your behaviour and you will come across as being needy (Arp, 2014). However, if your date is to get to know someone, then you probably come across as being a bit interview-oriented. Your safest bet is to consider dating as a chance of having fun. This will keep you date honest and interesting in getting to know you more and what having fun with you really feels like. Most guys often likes being around fun-loving, warm-hearted, low-pressure people with no apparent expectations (FISMAN & IYENGAR, 2008). Gradually, you will become more familiar with each other's likes and preferences, becoming emotionally attached to someone and instantaneously telling them about your history during the first two are three dates' promises to me very catastrophic and will more than likely, suck the fun out of the casual encounter. It is very possible that to compare this to giving away the surprise of the hidden object in a present before they unwrap it. Always focus on having fun, make the best out of every date, enjoy the mystery, then and only then, will the transition from a casual to a serious relationship transfers naturally (Arp, 2014).

SIGNS OF A SERIOUS RELATIONSHIP

There are clear signs to look for when trying to figure out if you're graduating from a casual dating relationship into a serious one. The dating process is complex and can be very tedious at times but if it all goes well, you won't need to ponder too long on ascertaining whether or not you're heading into a serious relationship (Anderson, 2013). There are a lot of hints and clue to get you in the know, this book has coined the most common ones and place them in a comprehensive manner for you reading pleasure. We coined them as milestones; these are specified points in a relationship where you become clear that it is official whether are not you verbally say is a relationship (Arp, 2014).

UNSCHEDULED TIME TOGETHER

When the feelings becomes so real, that you starts spending time together without even making or clearing your schedule then you know that you are getting serious about making it official (Arp, 2014). The same is true for your significant other. If he cancel work or a game with the guys just to hang with you then that's a clear hint that you are getting his main attention (Arp, 2014).

MEETING HIS FRIENDS

There's only a few things a guy cherish more than his buddies, his car his house and his woman. Whenever he takes you to see, meet and greet his friend then you know he's no longer messing around. Meeting each other's friends and or social group is one of the hugest steps a potential couple can ever take. If you are lucky enough to make it past the excruciating stages of scrutinizing friends, then things are well on their way (Arp, 2014).

SLEEPOVERS WITHOUT SEX

Having a sense of trust for your partner not only speaks volumes of your growth into a stable relationship but a stunning transformation from a casual to serious one. Being able to trust have a lot to do with longevity in relationship that far outweighs the pleasures of having sex (Hobbs, 2008). This also shows that you partner think more of you than just to be his pleasure bunny but as a source of comfort and accompaniment he can rely on. As long as you are involved in constant confrontation then you are well on your way in the transition process (Hobbs, 2008).

HE LEAVE SOME STUFF AT YOUR HOUSE

The most impressive sign of a real relationship going steady is when you have to keep picking up his stuff and packing them away for him in your home. It means that he is now comfortable with you as his main lady and is planning on committing, If leaves a pair of boxers at your place more than once, then he's giving you a hint (Arp, 2014). Conversely, if he gives you a drawer at his apartment or ask s you to give him one of yours then you know that you've hit the jackpot (Arp, 2014).

SIGNS OF A SERIOUS RELATIONSHIP CONT'D

THE BIG ONE: YOUR FIRST FIGHT

People often view couple squabble as all negative, however, this is not always the case, many fights stands to prove just how committed a guy is to a relationship and rather to fuss it out than just giving-in and calling quits. If you have a fight and it doesn't result in you breaking up, it stands to prove that you both think that what you share is something worth fighting for (Bettie, 2008). This is one of the most significant of all the signs. The one who stuck with you through the storms and the draught is the one most deserving to be there to ride with you through the smooth patches (Arp, 2014).

Once you have spotted at least three of these hints, then you know you are heading for a serious relationship, don't panic, remain calm and allow things to play out. The worst thing you can do at this point is to push things beyond extraordinary limits (Anderson, 2013). To help encouraged this transition, you could also drop a few hints of your own and see if he catches on. Never let your-self seem to be too desperate. Allow yourself and your partner, enough time to adjust to the status of a serious relationship. The key is being attentive and proactive and don't get caught trying to force the issue. Once again, if he loves you today, he will love you tomorrow just the same (Anderson, 2013).

SIX FIRST TIMERS IN MOVING FROM CASUAL TO SERIOUS

There are a plethora of things that women do for the first time when moving from casual to permanent relationships, the key is getting a working knowledge of these activities and ensuring that you are aware of these signs when they present themselves (Anderson, 2013). Men also do things for ladies on first instances that they don't normally do. Here now is a detailed listing of most of the first-timers that most males and females go through:

1. The First Time You Spend A Night In Together

The smooth transition from a casual affair to a serious commitment could be characterized by the first time you spent a romantic Friday night together either in the privacy of his own home, the evening may or may not include sexual exchanges but it sure will include romancing (Arp, 2014).

2. The First Time You See Each Other "Au Naturel"

Truth is, you may have been seeing each other naked on multiple occasions, however, it is quite sensible to note that these exchanges might have been aided by the covert obstruction of the sheets, pillows and dim-lighting and the natural looking touch-ups that you so cheekily re-and in the bath room. However, seeing each other for the same with clear visuals, the un-brushed and un-kept hair, the blemished and dried skin, the awkward shape of his relaxed manhood, and for women a day without makeup would be you worst but he as seen you with it and he still hasn't call it quits, it means you're pretty comfortable with each other (Arp, 2014).

3. The First Time You Call Just To Talk

Males rarely calls just to talk, they always have some hidden agenda up their sleeves. Whenever a male calls genuinely to just have a sincere talk with you with no strings attached then that's him dropping a first time hint of how he feels. Maybe you could return the favour by calling him about something else such as scheduling a date, asking about a plan of interest etc. whatever the reason, but once this information is exchanged, you don't need to immediately end the call, instead you build and extend the conversation. There and then you'll find you have a lot of issues to talk with each other about, and before you realize, you've been on the phone for more than an hour or two. This is not just physical but you two are heading for a serious relationship (Arp, 2014).

SIX FIRST TIMERS IN MOVING FROM CASUAL TO SERIOUS CONT'D

4. The First Time You See Each Other Really Drunk

You accompany him to a night-out, he overdo it, you warned him as you know he hold his liquor, he gets drunk and you take him home, he gets sick with an hang-over, he then gets sad and apologize before passing out...and you still like him when you wake up and see him fast asleep in bed the next morning. That's how you know that you are in a serious relationship (Arp, 2014).

5. The First Time You Talk about Your Exes

It has become a universally accepted law not make mention of your ex on the first (or second, or even the third) date, however, this subject is bound to come about some time in the future and the first time you talk about it can be a very awkward time for you both (FISMAN & IYENGAR, 2008). Talking about his exes and dating history indicates that he cares about you enough to tell you all the highs and lows of his dating history. Everyone knows not to mention an ex on a first (or second, or third) date, but eventually the subject is bound to come up. Talking about each other's exes and dating histories shows that you care about a person enough to hear all the gory details of their dating life (Arp, 2014).

6. Seeing Each Other Sick for the First Time

No one likes to see a love one sick, no matter how cruel or heartless they have been to us. Often times, a person feeling sick may be tired, vulnerable, and crabby and to an extent gross. Allowing you boyfriend to see you in such states requires a new level of commitment to stay grounded. If that person is not turned off by your condition and is willing to assists in nursing you back to health, then you know that your relationship is serious (Arp, 2014).

Now you have a full and working knowledge of what to look for when getting serious and all the mental process involved in preparing to go exclusive (Washburn & Christensen, 2008). Be warned that you may need to slow down the pace at which you run into this stage, you can never know too much about your partner (Arp, 2014). Take your time to get to know all there is to know about him (Uprety & Adhikary, 2008). Ensure that you are never at alas for any significant information about him. You should be able to care for him without consulting his family should he fall ill for a week, I you can't do this, then you are not ready to transition into anything serious with him (FISMAN & IYENGAR, 2008). We hope these words have made you into better individual daters and aide you in making safer dating decision.

CHAPTER 10:
Virtual Dating! Is It Safe?

"It's kind of freaky to send your picture over the Internet to someone you don't really know and then have to sit waiting for their judgement on how you look. Maybe that's why my aunt, Penny, who got divorced two years ago, hates online dating so much. Mom's always nagging her to go back on Match.com but Aunt Penny says she'd rather have root canal work - without anaesthetic."

—Sarah Darer-Littman

TRADITIONAL VS ONLINE DATING

T he hassles involved in finding the love of your life can be a daunting process, and the journey can often be a lonely one with infuriating experiences often characterize by rejection and uncertainty. The use of electronic devices such as iPhones, tablets and PC, has been able to ease the process somewhat, with the heralding of online dating. This facility allows you the access of searching for romance and companionship from the comfort of your own home (Epstein, 2007). The verdict is out, and we've realized that no system is without error, though it has been seen as very convenient, we must point out that online dating has great benefits and equally great degree of danger. We now consider the major differences that exist between traditional and online dating (Epstein, 2007).

SEARCHING

It is quite remarkable and true that except you get hooked up with a friend of your friend or you get acquainted with someone at work, the process of physically searching for someone to go out with often entails frequenting malls or other public-social meeting point in a attempt to find your soul mate (Epstein, 2007). Sparking a conversation with someone new is not a walk in the park and can be very awkward and even embarrassing at times which may even reduce your chance of success. Conversely, online dating allows the freedom of browsing the personal profiles of potential mates in the ease and comfort of your home thereby reducing the stress and pressure involved in the traditional means. Here, you are at total liberty to choose the duration of your browsing experience, the time of the day you want to browse, and where (location) in the world you want to search, this provides you with dating on your own terms (Ellison, 2003). Nevertheless, it should be understood that being exposed to so many options, can be extremely daunting especially for an inexperienced dater. The experience for many can become very impersonal and displeasuring with the absence of instant attraction and the atmosphere that one often feels when meeting new prospect in a physical dating setting (Epstein, 2007).

SELECTIVITY

With online dating, you are required to upload a personal photograph in addition to a plethora of additional information, including but not limited to, career aspirations, your hobbies, personal tastes and preferences in movies, TV shows, food and men (Ellison, 2003). In you choose to interacted with a certain predefined set of individuals, you may be doing so based on much more than just a mere attraction or crush on someone, you are also doing so based on the added information supplied which may help to reduce the challenge of sparking a real face-to-face conversation with a potential mate, here you already know a few things about the person so it's easier to move forward from that. Conversely, the traditional means of dating often induces a little more determination, conviction and assurance, which often times than not results in greater emotional processes. This form of dating however, allows you the freedom of getting to know you potential partner slowly over a longer period of time (Epstein, 2007). This will enable an induced element of mystery and suspense, thereby allowing for fun-filled future discoveries

TRADITIONAL VS ONLINE DATING CONT'D

SCOPE

Most females often turn to online dating as a remedial action to their immediate economic or social worries. It may be that their current employment career and or social circles have little or no room to allow them the freedom of dating in physical spaces on a regular basis. With the emergence of online dating, females now have a wider scope in the number of potential partners to choose from (Epstein, 2007). This have then increased the possibility of allowing you to search for romance within several spheres, whether locally or internationally, within a town, within a certain social group, political or spiritual club or even from specific interest segments. This widened scope can serve both as a benefit and as a pitfall in that, searching for a perfect partner in a defined region can be hard as is, therefore, extending the search to include the entire globe may result in a rather strenuous and excruciating process of finding love. Furthermore, getting acquainted with someone who lives thousands of miles away may result in logistical challenges, such as exorbitant travelling expenses to entail when meeting with your partner which are not necessarily present in the traditional dating process (Epstein, 2007).

MISREPRESENTATION

It must be understood that the disclosure of completely accurate information online is a scarce commodity. Though many guys are untruthful in the traditional dating process, online dating has drastically increase the prospect of supplying misrepresented information as there is no tamper proof mechanism available to ward against these practices on cyber dating sites (Epstein, 2007). Dishonest men, posing as honest daters are at liberty to use fake names, and or outdated or unreal profile photos with exaggerated special effects in a bid to lure unsuspecting female admirers. These men will even beef-up their profile histories and create fabricated stories that speaks to the audiences emotions that they hope to attract. Be warned that not all you see online is as it seems, there are bi-sexual, trans-genders, crossdressers, gays and lesbians who withhold these information from the unsuspecting dater, which may be catastrophic later on if you are not into certain sexual orientations (Arp, 2014). The advice to you is that you should do extensive background research on these online profiles before going out on dates and or excursions. Conversely, traditional dating allow for less anonymity, here, you'll have an idea whether or not you are dealing with a real person, alongside engaging in personal face-to-face conversation, thereby limiting exaggerated physical description or fabricated personality types. The use of online technology is somewhat static, hence with traditional dating you have an opportunity to solicit the opinion of friends and love ones which is less likely with online dating sites.

TRADITIONAL VS ONLINE DATING CONT'D

CONSIDERATIONS

Compared to traditional dating, online dating provides an additional shield of protection not available in the physical dating environment. Here, the physical space may be your bed, on a flight, in your kitchen, on a vacation or maybe even your care but the date occurs in cyber space, thereby eliminating the physical hassle of travel and meet (Hobbs, 2008). Here, you are not at liberty to meet the your online date until you are completely comfortable and secure in the fact that he is a real gentleman with stunning qualities and you can trust him completely . In terms of increased security measures while utilizing online dating sites, be sure not to exchange personal contact information until you are superbly convinced that you are dating a trustworthy and honest man (Arp, 2014). Moreover, If all things goes well and you think that you can trust him enough to exchange contacts and eventually setup a physical date, then make certain that your initial date is setup within public spaces and that some close family and or friend knows of your whereabouts and the time you are scheduled to return, if needs be, ask them to give you one are two calls throughout the date, just to ensure that you are okay. Places like restaurants, café or shopping mall are quite crowded and is often a good place to have that first date, consider these spaces before opting for anywhere else that may be too intimate (Epstein, 2007). These rules are not skewed only to online dating but to traditional dating scenarios as well, more so if the guy was someone you met at a random bar are somebody you share little or no social interactions with. Always be safe, be in charge, be adorable, and be loved.

THE DOs AND DON'Ts OF ONLINE DATING

Except your career lies within an environment that is totally dominated by male professional, for example, an architectural department, urological disorder office, on the NASCAR race track, or on the construction site, your search for your ideal mate will more than likely take you to the internet. A good thing to note is that the internet is always crawling with men, who are also searching for love money, attention or a one night stand as well. Therefore, you must be prepared to commit long hours and high levels of mental efforts, in a bid to comprehend the pervasive nature of online dating and learning how to separate the sheep from the goats. We now provide you with a short discourse on the dos and don'ts of online dating, as we try to get you up-to-date in knowing what to do and what not to do online (Epstein, 2007).

DO be sure to post an updated picture, providing an authentic sketch of your attributes, virtues and personality. A guy once went on a popular dating site, and began drooling after seeing the picture of a dazzling bikini-clad, brunet model. After numerous messages and correspondence over the internet and cell-phone he went on a physical date, expecting to see the scrumptious beauty he had been communing with online, only to meet a divinely obese woman in a smashing tank-top and matching jean, he was devastated. He was so depressed that he drank two shots of tequila before passing out. Conversely, lying about your appearance will only hurt you in the long run when all shall be revealed. Be honest to you self and see, maybe they'll be grateful enough to go out on a second date (Epstein, 2007).

DON'T be fooled into thinking his picture is and will be as up-to-date and as genuine (without retouches) as yours do. It is quite possible to accept a dating invitation from a man you thought had the face of Prince Charming and the body of a Greek god, However, you may have never stopped to think that in actuality, he may be resembling the Great Dracula, with a mouthful of rotten teeth and pointy ears to match. Never underestimate the corrective power of Photoshop (Epstein, 2007).

DO get acquainted with universal jargons for online dating profiles. Here are a few to lookout for:

He says: "I'm cuddly."
True Meaning: "I'm chubby"
He says: "People tell me I'm quite handsome."
True Meaning: "My mother tells me I'm quite handsome"
He says: "I'm the Chief Executive Officer for a Major Industrial Corporation."
True Meaning: "I'm self-employed in my own home-based business"

THE DOs AND DON'Ts OF ONLINE DATING CONT'D

DON'T become overly flustered upon the use of a few catchy lines, worn-out catch phrases like, "Heaven must be missing an angel, because you are divinely formed and structured." Be very wary of the friendly strangers who promises, "I will snuggle up with you in front of the fireplace" and "enjoy sunset strolls on the beach." These are popularly rehearsed lines and they come from the mouth of men who have only a single intent, and that's to get you in bed. That the reasons why they sound so good in your ear, seems they may have taken a course in "What women loves to her 101" beware (Epstein, 2007).

DO If he sounds astute and collegial; improve on your arithmetic to be safe:

- Minus 3inches from his height.
- Multiply his weight by two.
- Divide his income by two
- Increase his age by at least ten years

DON'T base your selection of a date online solely on photographs. It is extremely effortless to scoot through the celebrities' online profile and select photo-lookalikes and make up the rest of information to suit the potential unsuspecting mate. In recapping, understand that real men often suffer from hair loss and often times replace them with fakes, notwithstanding, if you happen to meet these guys in person, you may never know the difference and may even be very attracted to them. Consequently, you may must you're your choices on the inward qualities that will last even with the muscles and the skin loses their function and becomes obsolete (Epstein, 2007).

DO, when the time is right, transition your conversation from dating site to email to cell-phone. You will find that some people are great at texting and writing emails (or even have a personal ghost writer for their profile) but as soon as the conversation moves to oral communication, we start developing challenges. Talking on the phone with your potential mate will provide you with a clearer sense as it relates to matching personality. Additionally, you will be gifted the first hand chance to decide whether or not he has a personality to begin with. Please be reminded that's if the conversation becomes boring and lacklustre, then it is an indication of what to expect in future phone calls (Bettie, 2008).

DON'T be drawn into the relaying of your home, school or work address without first building a high level of trust with him. The disclosure of personal information that could be traced back to your address, such as last name, email address that includes your last name or your home phone credential is strongly ill-advised. Most men using online dating forum are as human as you are, however, some are not. You wouldn't want Freddy Cougar standing at your door with a box Godiva creamy cakes, regardless that they are ruffles (Epstein, 2007).

THE DOs AND DON'Ts OF ONLINE DATING CONT'D

DO remember to take baby steps in getting to know your online dating buddy. The chemistry may be really great between you now and he gets your and can relate to everything your feeling especially when you're feeling down, still proceed cautiously and very slowly. Some people are very good actors and only time can pull the veil from your eyes and show you who they really are so no rush, take your time (Arp, 2014). When planning on meeting him for the first time, once again let me again stress that you meet him in a public space for at least the first two or three first dates. As you begin to know more about him, then you may start consider asking him to pick you up and drop you off at your home. The point to remember is never to invite him in until after the 10th or even the 12th date. At that point you will be more than able to understand what he is like and most players would have given up by then. Until then, don't invite him in, even if he tells you he's having cramps and needs to use your bathroom (Epstein, 2007).

DON'T act childish in your use off online chatrooms, temptations will present themselves on your dating sites, control the pages you visit and don't be lured into online pornography and hot and steamy webcam chats, seize and desist from these practices if you already find yourself involved (Arp, 2014). Additionally, online dating has the same principles as traditional dating, therefore, if you are dating a guy online who you think sincere, kind and honest, and you have been experiencing a good time since you met, then don't run to your computer every few minutes to flirt with other guys online because you think they are hot. It is easy to get distracted on the internet with the plethora of handsome guys just screaming for your attention, if you keep this up, then you would have soon lost sight of what was important and get played by pretentious suiters (Epstein, 2007).

CHAPTER 11:
Re-entering the Dating Pool

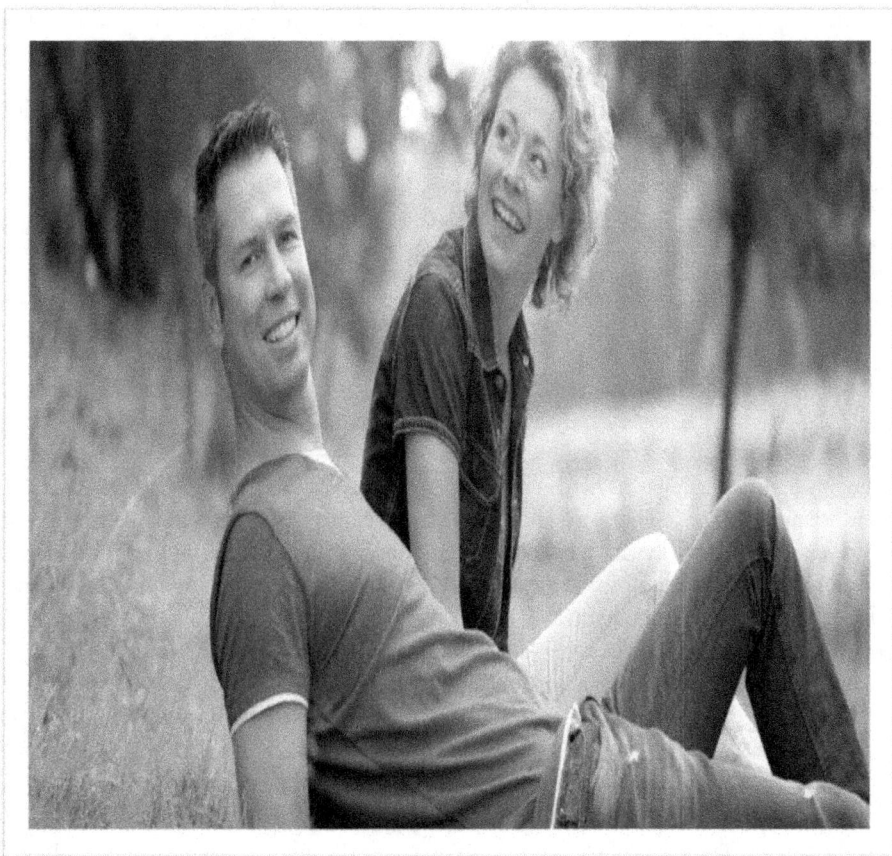

"Wine comes in at the mouth And love comes in at the eye; That's all we shall know for truth Before we grow old and die."

— William Butler Yeats

HOW TO RE-ENTER THE DATING POOL

Geneva is a single mom who is recently divorce. She has decided to wait until her daughter is fully grown before re-entering the dating scene, however, she still has a few challenge in charting the way forward. "I want to date again but I will only do so when Jada is out of the house but I don't know how to do it"

Angela is divorced for less than a year now and stays at home to care for her two sons who are still in kindergarten school, however she'd like to re-enter the dating pool again, like Geneva, and she needs some advice in charting the way forward whilst making the dating process easy on her kids.

Anthony is currently separated from his marriage to Janise. Anthony would like to re-enter the dating pool again, his friends thinks this is true as he has become a bit grumpy since the split, after-all, he's going to be getting a divorce within a couple of weeks. However, Anthony is wary of the ramifications of such actions as he's still legally married and dating now would only complicate things further.

Geneva's, Angela's and Anthony's concerns are common issues among women and men today. According to the U.S. Census Bureau, 19.3 million of US citizens are in the process are will be getting a divorce each year, many people just rush out of one marriage, date and re-enter another and then start the process all over again. Maybe you are currently sharing the concerns of the three case scenarios given as you additionally ponder on how if ever you will be able to re-enter the evasive world of dating. This book provides a few practical ideas to help.

When one becomes accustomed to consistently waking up in the morning and kissing the same gently lips every day for years, you don't just forget about that person after a divorce. Waking up a couple of mornings or two without the one you once loved can be a hard pill to swallow for the newly divorced (Arp, 2014). Furthermore, the added pressure of re-entering the dating pool after many years of feeling safe, loved and security, it's no mystery that you are feeling over the edge right now. Nonetheless, the process of re-entering the dating pool after many years of commitment doesn't have to be as traumatic as most people allow it to be (Nerdlove, 2011). Choosing online dating niches, such as professional/faith-based virtual communities like JDate.com, Match.com and ChristianMingle.com may not be such a bad idea for the newly single daters. These virtual communities allow new singles the freedom of having a varied nature of options from which to choose like-minded matches who shares the same core values and principles. Having a common interest, footing or platform with a match from the very onset is a great indication of a good, healthy and meaningful relationship (Bettie, 2008). So whether you're newly single or you've just made up your mind to date again, here are five things you need to as you embark on your journey into the dating pool:

BE SURE YOU'RE READY

The emotional processes of dealing with separation from your lover by death or divorce can be extremely challenging, and entering the dating arena too early after suffering these setbacks can be catastrophic. Prior to agreeing on going out again (on a date), be sure you are emotionally ready to deal with the inclinations of meeting other singles and being interested to enter into casual relationships with them should the possibility arises. Do not go out on a date if you find yourself breaking down emotionally after doing certain activities you would have only shared with your previous partner (Arp, 2014). Dating should always be fun and exciting, so engage the process with a positive outlook if you want it to work.

HOW TO RE-ENTER THE DATING POOL CONT'D

KEEP AN OPEN MIND

Keeping an open mind when re-entering the dating scene is critical. You would have been quite knowledgeable of your likes and preference by this time when it comes to men. However, this doesn't give you a safety cushion so as to say that life won't surprize you every other time you go out on a date (Bettie, 2008). They key is to continuously learn new ways and terminology to deal with certain issues. You are only limited by yourself when you look for only people with your previous class of men; maybe that was why you ended up in this place at first (Nerdlove, 2011). It narrow minded to seek companionship from individual criteria such as superman, or someone with a master's degree. Rather, compile a draft of the significant virtues and attributes you hope for in a perfect match and the leave room for adjustments (Ellison, 2003).

DON'T COMPARE

It is pointless to attempt to equate yourself with others around you. Following the norm and trying to mirror others will only leave you in tatters. Trying to analyse all the married people around you and acting accordingly will only make you feel even worst about your failed attempts at relationships and even marriage. Experience is the best teacher, therefore, learn from you mistakes and try not to make those same choices that resulted in your previous downfall (Arp, 2014). The advice for you is to be yourself and demand what you need, never settling for mediocrity or half-hearted commitment. Allow your new relationship to blossom without any interference from your previous relations, therefore do not try to compare him with you ex. everyone has different traits and personality and therefore should be judge solely on their own merits and not that of you past husband or boyfriend (Arp, 2014).

PLAY IT SAFE

If you are going back into the dating pool with the aid of online infrastructure or through the aid of a good friend, hooking you up with another friend i.e. online or offline, then you need to make safety your very first priority (Arp, 2014). Going out with some new for the first time after marriage can be challenging, and for most women, this is the point when they start to trust someone else to take care of their emotional needs other than there previous partner. This is especially burdensome for women who find it hard to trust again after being hurt multiple times. Your first date after a divorce or separation, like any other first dates, must be done within the confines of public spaces. Choose a public setting and provide for your own transportation to and from the venue. Also remember that before you leave for a date, you must tell a friend or close family member where you're headed to and ask them to give you one or too calls during the date to ensure you are okay (Epstein, 2007).

HOW TO RE-ENTER THE DATING POOL CONT'D

GET YOUR FRIENDS INVOLVED

Good friends are priceless. Often times, your friends provides the greatest moral support you'll ever need to get back into the dating pool (Epstein, 2007). They are there when you're feeling down and out and they will cheer you on as you take the first steps back to normalcy. They are there for you, used them as you moral support, and ask them to help you in your time of need or whenever you need a shoulder to lean on. When trying out online for the first time, ask your friends for their advice, ask your brother, your sister, you mom, your dad or even your kids for help (if they are old enough and are in support of your new transition into the dating world whenever you need help setting up your online profile (Epstein, 2007). They can serve as your profile curators and assist you in choosing the best pictures that show off all your stunning beauty and denote the real you choose the best pictures of yourself to show the real you!

NB: Kids are often the hardest hit in a breakup or divorce, support them as best as you can and hold off dating for as long as possible until you feel both you and your kids are ready to welcome someone new in your lives. The five tips provided will aide in allowing you to avoid most if not all dating pitfalls and or catastrophe. The dating process can be strenuous at times; however, you ensure that the fun outweighs the anxiety. It is okay to harbour the feeling of your first flirtation, allow yourself to get absorbed in the romantic vibe of your first phone call (Epstein, 2007). Bear in mind that you will be involved in a date that will probably end less than unsatisfactory, however, you are going to meet a few awesome people as well. The key is learning how to take each date as they come and find a way to enjoy every experience. Surround yourself with positive people that will help you whenever you need emotional support and enjoy yourself no matter what happens (STRAUS, 2004).

DIVORCE IS NOT THE END-TAKE HEART

The experiences of re-entering the dating world can be bi-fold by newly single women, they may see it as an exciting and glorious opportunity to rekindle their engrossed fetish or they might view it as intimidating (Ellison, 2003). However, it is natural for women to feel the need for companionship as soon as a month or two after their divorce. Statistics have shown that almost 50% of American marriages end in divorce each year, when compare to those getting married. Quite a staggering figure but the fact is that people change over time, and with personal changes and preferences comes changes and preferences in partners as well (Nerdlove, 2011). Previously, we gave you five tips on what to do when re-entering the dating pool, we now will consider five more things to do before jumping back into the dating pool. To truly love someone, you must first love yourself and to love yourself you must first know yourself, taking careful time to explore and understand yourself as a single individual can never be over emphasise. This will help you to find happiness and satisfaction in your new partner (US Stats, 2013).

INDULGE IN SELF-DISCOVERY

Being single again may be a blessing in disguise, giving you a second chance at learning new things about yourself. Discover new ideas, new horizon, new philosophies, and new places and spaces in your personality which will not only make you into a better person but prepare you for what you will need to be a better partner in the future. Allow relationship tears and spoils caused from the divorce to heel naturally without force or any form of inducements before entering into any form of new relationships (Nerdlove, 2011). Your self-esteem and emotional stability can be greatly affected by a divorce so ensure that your self-esteem is intact as well checking to see that your emotions are stabilized before heading into any new relationships. Here, you first need to accept that you are hurting, and then further accept that it is okay to feel hurt, however this is where it ends, do not dwell on the past. Use every bad experience as a stepping stone to greater things. Therefore you must learn to take care of yourself before attempting to taking care of others. You are important, pamper and nurture your mind, body and soul as you embark on new beginnings (Nerdlove, 2011).

GRIEVE WITH YOUR KIDS

As mentioned earlier, you must allow yourself and family time to grieve over the loss of a dad or step-day whether through death or separation and preparing for a new one (Washburn & Christensen, 2008). Not dating during the time of the serration or tragedy will allow your family enough time to adjust to the new possibilities of life without dad, this will also discourage you from making impulsive mistakes that may be hard to correct after the fact. Reports have shown that 9 out of 10 rebound relationships are less likely to turn into healthy relationships and may even further delay the healing process (Nerdlove, 2011). If you are a single mom with children coping from divorce, then it is expedient that you provide then with sufficient time to face the facts of the situation before bringing new people into their lives (Nerdlove, 2011). Always proceed to dating at your own pace, never rush the issue and care for others around you. Build new social circles to combat lonely evenings and resist the feelings of depurations as they come (Bettie, 2008).

DON'T LOWER YOUR EXPECTATIONS

Resist the temptation that you need to settle for mediocrity when looking for a partner, you deserve the best of everything. Always approach the horizon thinking that this is your chance for a fresh start (Bettie, 2008). You didn't get divorce so you could live a life of hurt and pain all over again so it's okay to be picky, take your time and discover first what you want in your next potential partner. Make a list of all the qualities that your spouse never had, and ensure that you shortlist prospects who are rich in those qualities and more. The process of dating will now help you to look for the traits and virtues you've always wanted in the perfect mate (Nerdlove, 2011). Be mindful of previous heartache and or insecurities, however never allow the past to determine the future, go for what you need and don't settle for less. The major advantage of dating is that you can stop seeing a guy who does not reach up to your expectation with minimal fuss. Therefore it is important that you set high expectations within the realms of reality (Bettie, 2008).

EXPLORE YOUR RESOURCES

The myriad of new opportunities out there are endless, the onus is on you however, to find your ideal guy by using the resources available to you. There are many different new resources, topologies and facilities at your fingertips to find that one true person that makes you happy and take your breath away, make use of them (Bettie, 2008). Online dating is one such topology which allows single mom, busy people and the timid hearted the opportunity of dating while balancing a job, the home and hyperactive children, and everything in-between (Nerdlove, 2011). Setting up your online profile should be easy. When setting up an online profile, it is advised that you expressly specify what you want in a bid to find the ideal candidate, don't leave out a think. It is also strongly advised that you are open-minded, that you are optimistic, and that you are accepting throughout this period of dating. Never allow mismatched dating error get you down. Remember that there are millions of other single men out there just waiting for the opportunity meet a woman like you (Ellison, 2003).

LEARN FROM PAST MISTAKES

A plethora of women divorcees found themselves being shelf-shocked at repeating the same mistakes when resuming dating. They fear they may become victim to the very same old pattern of character traits they thought was the perfect match and ultimately choose the wrong person for a second time (Bettie, 2008). The advice is that you retrieve the pieces of your life that have gone in tatters and camper on to better days. Diversify your dating experience by dating guys who are not really your type in a bid to learn new personality traits and virtues that would work ideally for a long term relationship (Arp, 2014). Always take a few moments to flashback before making any ultimate decision in a bid to think about you options and choose wisely.

DIVORCE IS NOT THE END-TAKE HEART CONT'D

Disassociate yourself from guys who display the same distasteful personality traits that you found in your previous partner. Actualize yourself and apprise the new person your divorce status has fashioned you into making you better for the future (Nerdlove, 2011).

NEVER HARBOR ON FAILURE

Remove the word failure from your vocabulary and replace it with test. On the same note, don't think of you divorce as a failure but as a test which have given you a second shot at making amends (Bettie, 2008). Think of it also as an opportunity to grow into something marvellous. Instead of focusing on all the negatives, think of all the positives that it has brought to your marriage, in terms of a wonderful wedding ceremony, and great kids that you will always love, care for and protect. All ways look at the positives from every bad relationship and use them to create a brighter prospect for the future. Regardless of what people do, you are the only one with the power to instil happiness and joy into your own life through self-actualization (Stutzer & Frey, 2003). In short, rebuke your failures and forsake them, but embrace your success and cherish them as they bring hope for a brighter future and a grander relationship.

Objectives|

After Reading This Section, You Will Be Able
To Assess The Following

- Defining the nature of your relationship
- Making it permanent
- Understanding relationships after marriage
- Learning how to fortify the ties
- Learning how to make it last

CHAPTER 12:
Relationships & You: Defining the Scope

"A loving relationship is one in which the loved one is free to be himself — to laugh with me, but never at me; to cry with me, but never because of me; to love life, to love himself, to love being loved. Such a relationship is based upon freedom and can never grow in a jealous heart."

—Leo F. Buscaglia

DEFINING THE RELATIONSHIP

According to Dr Nerdlove, in her article "Ace the, 'Why are you not married?'," most women believes that the two most dreaded phrases that often infuse a sense of fear in the hearts of most men are the phrases "....We need to talk" and "...Where do you think this relationship is going?" The belief is that most men would rather provide answers to the questions of "How was your day at work today?" or "How's the new engine you installed performing so far?" The dreaded "Defining the Relationship" talk has always been met with intense nervousness, anxiety, distress and concern and many men (and women to a lesser extent) try to shy away from such discussion. Studies have shown that this talk often provide cognitive dissonance of the most highest proportions in men, predominantly because it almost always comes up in the most untimely situations. Here, this is the moment where you are suddenly expected to make a long term decision which will permanently affect your relationship both immediately and in the long-run. Nerdlove believes that this talk, for most men, indicates a significant immediate juncture, where a major and possibly undesirable decision may be required that may change the nature of their relationship with the person forever. Regardless that you wish to change the public nature of the relationship from casual dater to 'boyfriend,' it is a segment of the transitionary phase from anonymous to exclusivity, and is often rigged with much worry and concern with the possibility for either great success or dismal failure (Nerdlove, 2011).

The questions are often asked, "When is the right time to discuss exclusivity, should I wait for a month or is that too soon? "Will three months be too late, if I pop the question and he says no, then what? If I mistook his genuine candour for something more than what they were and thought he wanted something serious, how do I move on after asking the unobvious? Most men have issues with commitment, they often engage in constant dialogues about the highly commitment-bound women, those who want you to commit or exit. However, works both ways, and often can spell trouble either way especially if he is the 'excessively devoted boyfriend,' it can be mystifying when you just want to keep things casual (Nerdlove, 2011). It's not an easy walk in the park as you struggle with these dilemmas, especially if he's looking for something serious and you don't but you still want to maintain his friendship. How will you cope? The first thing you need to do is to calm down. The major cause of this cognitive dissonance is because we panic and do things based on impulsive actions and not based on proven advice. The key for success here is approaching these talks with clear level heads, an open mind and the willingness to talk things through to the end without getting disintegrated. Put less weight on the talk and more on the outcome, don't force the issue if you think the other person is a little pressured, the first signs of anxiety means that you are not ready for the talk and so you need to allow more time for your partner to develop the psyche to tackle this talk with the lest fuss and or strain (Nerdlove, 2011).

WHEN TO HAVE THAT TALK

Many women struggle with the basic challenge of when to ask the question of relationship status. Though it is good to have a tamper free guide and a set rule of thumb as to when to ask the question, for instance should I ask him three weeks after we start sleeping together, should I ask him after that 'killer' date where I feel really comfortable with him? However, there is no explicit wrong or right time to ask for the relationship status as all relationships are different and must be treated separately. Therefore, in all relationships, timing will be different; however, there are a few factors to consider that will give you an honest idea of when exactly it is okay for you to ask the question. Bear in mind that these guidelines varies from relationships to relationships and most be customized to suit your particular terms and preferences (Nerdlove, 2011).

HOW OFTEN HAVE YOU BEEN SEEING EACH OTHER?

As we learnt from the previous section, the process of dating is Dating is a snowballing involvement; therefore, how often you experience each other, will impact greatly on how soon or how long you wait to have that major discussion. According to Nerdlove, if you share a date with you partners once or twice per week (mostly on weekends when you're not working) then you are expected to be less likely comfortable at having that discussion anytime soon. Nonetheless, if you are a couple who engage in dating each other four to five times per week, (after work in the evenings) then there is a lot more probability that you will be more comfortable at having such a discussion (Nerdlove, 2011). Having constant intimate contact with your partner and seeing him on a regular basis means that you are, whether consciously or unconsciously, heading towards something more than just casual relations. It means that you are enjoying something which is more than just sex but rather recognizing that you see the possibility often starting and maintaining mutual exclusivity and can therefore invest in a relationship together (Nerdlove, 2011). Now more than ever, at this juncture, you should definitely take the initiative to 'pop' the question in discussing just where you think the relationship will be heading in the near and extended future. A point of caution though is to consider the amount of time you spend together to talk when you do get the opportunity to go out on a date. Getting together for four to five times per week after work and not spending prolonged periods together just to talk may mean that you should contemplate pushing this major discussion back until the point where you feel comfortable talking to each other about anything. Conversely, if you only see him in short instant intervals between moments of long non-contact where you hook-up for intimacy and sex, it is highly advised that you consider having the 'talk' sooner rather than later. The intervals of time spent together, coupled with the length of time spent apart, often determine the importance of ensuring that you both are on the same page.

WHEN TO HAVE THAT TALK CONT'D

HOW OFTEN DO YOU COMMUNICATE OUTSIDE OF YOUR DATES?

Most people believe that if you are crazy about someone, then the inclination is that you have to see them every day; this has never been so far from the truth. The presence of a need or longing to see your partner has been proven to be a catalyst for improving relationship's durability and potency. Moreover, the weekly or daily schedule of a partner might deny him the privilege of going out on dates with you on a regular basis. However, this does not add fuel to the argument that lack of physical contact means lack of communication and emotional involvement (Nerdlove, 2011). Note carefully however, that the volume of communication extended in a relationship will be critical in determining when to have the 'talk'. For a couple that involves in lengthy discussions every day over the phone or on social media even in the busy slots of their schedules, it is quite possible that they can have the major talk in defining their relationship as being exclusive. However, if a couple finds it hard to find time inside of their schedule to talk to each other where you are often busy and even late for dates, then it is only fair to assume that this couple will be better served talking things slow in defining the relationship. Here, this couple's mannerism is only reflective of the underlying fact that they are ineptly invested into the relationship and need more time to figure things out (Nerdlove, 2011).

ARE YOU HAVING SEX?

Having a measure of thumb, once you've slept together, it is already too late to define the relationship. Accord to Dr Nerdlove, it is very easy to roll with the punches as they come, as long as you haven't slept together. The relationship will be considered as casual, as long as you haven't slept together, however, as soon as this line is breached and you become sexually involved, the relationship will become more complicated. The safest and most secure advice is to wait for whatever reason it may be, whether for a sense of assurance, moral conviction or religious persuasion, it is always advised to institute your expectations from the onset. The bad guys are less likely to stick around if they don't have a clear view of when they will be allowed access to your 'goodies'. However, those guys who are willing to stick with you are often the good ones and are more likely to commit and build a mutually exclusive relationship. Most women in a relationship, characterized by uncertainty and sex, often find it difficult to have that talk with their partner for fear of rejection. The advice is that even though you are already late to have the talk, it is always better to be late in asking, than never asking at all. Here, you need to determine his expectations from the relationship and inform him of yours, especially if it becomes obvious to you that you are not on the same page. It is safer to know the status-quo and maintain honesty about how you feel rather than suffering regrets and disappointment because you hid your feelings and found out later you had differences in views in terms of exclusivity (Nerdlove, 2011).

WHEN TO HAVE THAT TALK CONT'D

NB: A rule of thumb is to know that if he has repeatedly refused to discuss exclusivity, then it is safe to say you are not exclusive. It is unwise and ill-advised to assume the notion of perceived commitment means that you are exclusive. Full commitment on your end does not validate full-fledged commitment on his part. For most women, exclusivity is critical, and if you feel the same way then you should express this sentiment from the initial stages of the dating process. If you procrastinate, then you run the risk of getting hurt in the latter stages of your relationship, regardless of your initial intentions (Nerdlove, 2011).

SCHEDULING THE TALK

Ⅰt is quit fascinating to think just how defensive some men gets when you mention that you think it time we had the talk without presenting some prior warnings. This, however, is the most cynical, uncanny and senseless way of negotiating a topic as important as the scope of your futures together. This method of transition will only serve to place him under the microscope and under increased tussle to offer a correct response immediately which will be binding for the entire duration of your lives together. "We've been going out for so long now Derrick, are you planning on committing to me or what?" This is utterly distasteful and may put your partner in the gritty position of feeling that he has little or no options but to commit there and then or risk the possibility of a breakup, leading to antipathy (Bettie, 2008). You wouldn't want to feel as if you were tricked into making a long term decision without adequate contemplation. Neither would you want to commit to someone you don't totally love because you were caught up in the moment. Defining the relationship is a significant discussion and therefore should not be taken lightly. Therefore, it is strongly advised that you sufficient time is provided for both party to carefully consider their options and the consequences of making each (Bettie, 2008).

Be descriptive in your initial approach; tell your partner that you would like if you both could have a comfortable conversation about your relationship together as well as figuring out where you both would like to see your selves in the near and extended future and what it might means to all the parties involved. You might want to go further and choose a mutual free time where you can meet face to face. Never discuss exclusivity over the phone. Choose a day when you're free from any other form of commitment, deadlines, or responsibility that may detract from fully discussing the extremity of the decision to be made. Choose a venue where you can both be relaxed and feel free to be yourself (Arp, 2014). Whether brief or extended, the conversation should be guided in such a way where both party is able to share his/her feelings and not be pressured into providing an immediate answer. If he is the initiator of the conversation and do so without warning, you are allowed to ask for additional time to think things through and suggest an alternative day to talk about it. The key here is that, you will know whether or not he cares about your feelings based on his response. If he respects you, then he gives you sufficient time to think and be happy that you want to take the time to think things through. Conversely, if he demands an immediate response, it shows that he is less concerned about your feelings and more about getting a response. This is a bright red-flag and you therefore need to proceed cautiously (Arp, 2014).

DEFINE YOUR TERMS

The major cause of challenges in exclusive relationships is the fact that couples fail to listen and comprehend each other in a cohesive manner. The challenge here is a matter of superiority and inferiority in relationships, here one partner may consider himself as being more educated of financially stable than the other. This holds true when one consider having that major talk in a bid to determine the relationship. Just the same as you differ from your partner is the same exact way that our mental process differs, therefore, it should not be assumed that your partner knows the difference between a casual and an exclusive relationship, hence you must think of a comprehensive way of differentiating the two without seeming too condescending (Rosenfeld, 2012). To one man, casual relations may mean 'non-exclusive with sex only, while to others it may mean, "we only see each other on weekends without sex." Conversely, exclusivity to some men may mean intimacy, romance and sex, to others it may mean, "She's my girlfriend" while yet to some others it may mean "We are about to get married." It therefore leaves the notion of identifying clearly what you want from a relationship and communicating that to your partner (US Stats, 2013). The process of defining your relationship requires that you first define your terms.

Here, you want to ensure that what you want and how you see things is clearly communicated. It should be clearly established from the onset after deciding that he fits the bill of a perfect match, that you define what you expect to achieve from the relationship just to ensure that you are on the same page. When you say you want a causal relationship, be sure to explain to him, just what you mean by 'casual' don't leave him to assume what you mean. State what you expect of him as well as what they should expect of you, never sell yourself short (Nerdlove, 2011). Ask him to explain what casual means to him, if he believes it is non-exclusive which may or may not lead into a serious relationship later on. If you require a serious relationship, be sure to explain to him that this entails close and intimate involvement, as well as a full time commitment such as marriage, living together with kids, or that you only expect that you spend more intimate time together while living your lives with the future slightly undefined. Always ask questions to be sure, though stroppy at times, you must clarify the fussy details to ensure that all the issues are understood by both parties. This will result in fewer arguments and reduce the level of cognitive dissonance swirling around in your head (Stutzer & Frey, 2003).

STAND UP FOR YOURSELF

The immense effort exerted when prance upon with a significant decision such as going exclusive can be intense, specifically when you are place in the position to make an immediate decision which leaves you with the inclinations that your relationship is at stake. Regardless of the fact that you may have had good intentions in the initial stages, you may still feel as though one wrong answer may result in tatters. Here you may be left to think that your honest immediate opinion may be hurting the person you care so much about and derailing what you had going on and thought was a happy and successful relationship. Here, it is critical for you to set and enforce your boundaries. If you're in a relationship were you feel you were forced to make a choice to stay because you didn't want to hurt your partner's feelings then you are only hurting yourself in the process of creating a miserable life for your partner (Nerdlove, 2011). Consider your relationship as a partnership, where both parties contributes equal efforts to ensure that the relationship works and not one party trying to please the other at the expense of their own feelings. Here, you both must be able to negotiate terms and compromise where possible in an attempt to discover a plan that works for you both. Moreover, this means that efforts should levied at being flexible, opportunity cost is also applied to relationships, i.e. some other alternative must be given up for the sake of a future with your partner. Therefore you must decide what you can afford to give up for the sake of this relationship and to weight the outcome whether or not if it was worth the investment (Nerdlove, 2011).

Nonetheless, we all have predetermined expectations that must be met in order for a relationship to exist. Therefore, make these expectations obvious in the initial stages of the major talks; be honest and upfront with this information. If marriage is a definite must in the near future, then you must say this and be very explicit about it. Withholding vital information from your partner because you are worry it will chase him away now but if left for later, might allow him time to change his mind, is only a further recipe for disaster. If he can't accept your future plans of getting married and having kids then he's not the man for you. He will not change his mind later and you will only end up having and epic, more brutal split in the future (Nerdlove, 2011). Say what you want from your ongoing relationship and refrain from suppressing your thoughts because of a fear of being rejected. If your immediate future goal is exclusivity, let him know, and if he doesn't want that then let him go. If you are more comfortable with a casually relationship right now but nay be e=interested in something more serious in the future then let him know as well, if he can't stay with you casually then he doesn't deserve you exclusively. If you don't think you are relationship material and that you are not comfortable with a monogamy orientation then say so. He will have to make that decision to have a girlfriend with a polygamy orientation, and he won't be upset when he sees you with other men (US Stats, 2013).

STAND UP FOR YOURSELF CONT'D

Your terms should not be force, but be delivered in the mannerism of an offer; here he has full rights to accept or reject you offer or give a counter offer. Moreover, the same way you would like to be given the freedom of choice to choose the type of partner you are with is the very same way, you must allow him to choose his course going forward. Be explicit about your desires, likes and preferences, be sure to state your baggage if any and allow him to thoroughly think things through (Nerdlove, 2011). Tell him what is compromising as apart to what isn't. you must also be willing to compromise where possible and reject those where you cant. Sometimes it is very hard to stand up for yourself, because you know that once you stand up for what you want or need, you stand the chance of losing everything. However, it is better to be sorry now and safe later, so if he doesn't match you criteria, then safely walk away (Uprety & Adhikary, 2008). Here, you must be honest enough to admit that you wanted different things that just dint work well when aggregated (Nerdlove, 2011). This wouldn't work out in the long-haul so it was a good decision, you must keep telling yourself that the decision was the most accurate. It will be a sad tale at first especially if you really cared about the person; however, fundamental incompatibilities can never be overlooked and should not be placed against the cost of your happiness (Nerdlove, 2011). It's for the best to breakup if your major talk yield the result that you are incompatible together, your breakup will heal sooner than you think and your ex-partner may even thank you later for allowing them to see that they had a true match elsewhere. It's better to walk away if your DTR conversation shows that you won't work (Nerdlove, 2011). This may give you an opportunity to salvage that old friendship and move on with your life.

CHAPTER 13:
Taking Huge Steps-Tying the Knot

"There are few things more frightening to a man than giving away his heart. And there are few things more comforting to a man than to know the woman he gave his heart to, will protect it with her life."

—Fawn Weaver

STEPPING TOWARDS THE BIGGY

Julia's boyfriend of seven years Mark, proposed to her on the doorsteps of her three bedrooms apartment in Malibu California. He was so fund of her, he just couldn't imagine himself living without her in his life, unfortunately for Mark, Julia was inexperienced and unlearnt and feared making an intractable mistake hence she said no, much to Mark's displeasure. Four years after such a dismal experience, a now well learnt and slightly more courageous Julia said yes to her second boyfriend who proposed to her in the car while driving to work. Sadly for Julia, it wasn't to be, as Mark pulled-the-plug five months after he'd proposed. She was utterly confused and heartbroken, how could she have been so blind, how could she have fallen for this trick? Julia thought she was well prepared as she was well read and took several relationship classes in a bid to be ready when the next man "pop the question" "why did she see this coming?" she pondered. Like Julia, many women are left thinking that the universe is against them, they have failed miserably in reading the signs of a true commitment that may be head towards marriage. There is no quite tested and proven science to know exactly how to know that he is the one to 'tie the knot with, however, there are some criteria to use when deciding whether or not he fits the bill for a lifelong partner (Stutzer & Frey, 2003). Consider the following:

INTEGRITY

Finding and honing an impeccable character is hard and sometimes impossible. It's never easy to maintain a perfectly clean record and most men will work assiduously at hiding their flaws until after marriage. With the rapid increase in online dating, it often difficult in knowing if the person you're dating in this virtual community is just an idolized profile created by articulate word-play or the authentic replica of the person behind the screen. Integrity goes a far way in commitment and the onus is on you to ensure that he is factual a truthful about all his doings both past and present (Stutzer & Frey, 2003).

HONESTY

Before making the big step, it is assumed that you have gotten the chance to spend quality time with the person and you have learnt to trust them completely. This works by asking a few deeper open-ended questions (that does not only require a yes or a no answer) and researching to ensure that the answers provided are authentic. Ensure that he speaks the truth even when it is liable to cost him a great deal. Additionally, ensure that he is the same person in private as he is in the public's eyes; most people are excellent pretenders and are expert at putting up a front to prove that they are honest. However, careful research will prove otherwise. Be sure to ascertain whether or not, he's willing to make sacrifices for others before making any form of commitments (Stutzer & Frey, 2003).

STEPPING TOWARDS THE BIGGY CONT'D

MUTUAL RESPECT

The clearest signs of respect in a relationship is being able to trust and showing cutesy to your significant other. This should be a consistent attempt at aiming to show genuine love, affection and care towards the man in your life. Whenever you truly respect someone, it will show, there will be a little or no eye-rolling when conversing, cynicism when negotiating, sarcasm when frolicking, and disdain when sympathizing, or second guessing in decision making. Respect is not synonymous with admiring someone's attributes (Stutzer & Frey, 2003). If you admire a man because he is an eloquent speaker, it doesn't mean that you respect him entirely. Moreover, it possible to respect someone and disagree with them concurrently, therefore, you must ensure that what you share is actual respect and not a sense of agreement. Mutual respect occurs where you and your partner shares the same amount of esteem for each other (Stutzer & Frey, 2003).

CONTINUANCE

The full test of your meek intents will be tried in its entirety only when you approach the confines of your partner's personality, attitude and virtues head-on. Initially, it will be relatively easy to overlook the faults and flaws of your partner during the early stages of courting. Occasionally, you may even overlook the telling signs of a possible mismatch in terms of compatibility. This is probably due to a biological function where our bodies create feel good hormones to dampen the immediate effect of feeling sad based on unmet expectations. Conversely, once the relationship starts to blossom and you start taking a closer inspection of the likes and preferences you have, which are currently not being met, here, the oxytocin levels gradually recedes, and your discernment radically improves. Peradventure, and you find that he is incapable of showing affections, that he often interrupts you after realizing that he actually does not like to express affection, after the twentieth time she interrupts you, after discovering he avoids conflict despite the costs—love and respect can be a bit more difficult to come by (Stutzer & Frey, 2003).

Many women indulge in either of two things whenever they assume the role of becoming joint partners in a relationship. The first point is that most women assume that their male counterpart will forsake their previous inclinations as a result of the implied love he has for her. Secondly, most women believe that their magnanimous, and their high and rich in love demeanour will recompense for unmet expectations. This is greatly admirable but is really far from the reality of what is (Stutzer & Frey, 2003). Studies have shown that the weaknesses and incompatibility in terms of virtues and values will occasionally result in a consistent questioning of your decision to date the other party initially. Here, you may even become exasperated and inept at showing love which will eventually cause you to question the reason why you're dating in the first place. According to Dr Nerdlove, your willingness to show love and Love and esteem should never be dependent on whether or not your partner is great.

STEPPING TOWARDS THE BIGGY CONT'D

This is predominantly due to the fact that, the ideology of a mortal man being perfect is unheard of in this time and era. However, thought a perfect man who loves you unconditionally and respects you wholesomely is unchartered grounds for many men, there are some critical issues a woman should not ignore when thinking of committing to a lifelong relationship (Nerdlove, 2011). The weakness of continuously being untruthful to your spouse, the inert virtue of being a miser, a violent streak of increased abuse whether, orally, emotionally or worst, physically, are bountiful reasons for reconsider entering into any form of long term relationship with these men (Nerdlove, 2011).

MUTUAL AGREEANCE

The best element of a successful relationship is one that is characterized by a stream of mutual understanding and agreement. Here, you are required to express the gifts of love and compromise in a bid for your dreams to be realized. We must understand that the presence of continuous encouragement and advocacy is needed for a healthy relationship in the process of getting married (Stutzer & Frey, 2003). Healthy relationships are also characterized by mutual partners who are positively focussed on supporting and making sacrifices for each other in times of doubt. If a relationship only caters for the needs of one person, then there is a great presence of imbalance. Rarely do relationships move along a well-defined trajectory, therefore, the need as arise for us to constantly analyse our relationships as often as required, in a bid to determine whether or not it is heading in the desired direction or if it is destined for derailment (Stutzer & Frey, 2003).

ARE YOU READY FOR MARRIAGE

I t's a miraculous moment for you, that first time when the man of your dreams, goes done on one knee and asks you to marry him, you said yes without even a little hesitation and took his hand in yours while you both share a passionate kiss. Congratulations, you are now officially engaged! If anyone told you that you'd be in such a position today you would probably told them they were crazy, but here you are today, happily engaged. You've worked long and hard to get to this stage and now you are finally where you need to be (Nerdlove, 2011). The fact of the matter though, is to understand that all successful marriages consist of two equally tremendous individuals, who have set their sights on the reality of what could be and are now reaping the rewards. Here, they would have gone to great limits in getting ready to take the next steps. Before getting matter, there is a list of things you must do before transitioning into the matrimonial festivities (Nerdlove, 2011). Here now is a short discourse on a list of 20 things you must accomplish before running to tie the knot:

GET A BROKEN HEART

This sentiment may sound harsh, misleading or even a bit cliché, however, this holds true in many relationships. If you have never gotten a chance to get your heart broken, then it means that you are not experienced enough to get married. Having the opportunity to go through a harsh breakup, instils in women, the life lessons on how to deal with mishaps in a relationship as well as enabling one to learn from their mistakes as well as how to prevent that from ever happening again (Nerdlove, 2011).

EXPLORE THE PERVASIVE NATURE OF ELECTRONIC DATING

Explore the avenues of finding love, expanding your horizon and diversifying your search in a bid to ensure that you don't limit yourself to just those guys in your community or major town. Here you will be experienced in terms of varying tastes and preferences and be ready to critiques guys from diverse ethnic background (Stutzer & Frey, 2003).

ENSURE YOU DON'T MAKE SIMILAR MISTAKES

In retrospect, what have you done badly that you wish you could correct? Did you have a key role to play in the demise of your previous relationship? What evidence do you have to prove that you didn't take the relationship for granted? Have you been neglectful in your duties as a girlfriend and or fiancé? Challenging questions these are, and it's very important that we address them comprehensively before moving forward into a new relationship. Here you have a full view of all your flaws and short comings and can make better decisions next time round (Stutzer & Frey, 2003).

ARE YOU READY FOR MARRIAGE cont'd

YIELD TO THE FORCES OF LOVE AT LEAST TWICE

Here you are in the process of success and failure in a bid to find that one true person that makes you feel complete. In this process you are bound to fall in and out of love with some of your other partners, be prepared for this and make allowances for yourself; then and only then can you truly learn to love unconditionally. If you haven't fallen in and out of love at least twice, then you are not ready for marriage (Nerdlove, 2011).

CREATE A LIST OF MUST HAVES IN YOUR IDEAL RELATIONSHIP

Be prepared to handle deal breakers for potential relationships, if a guy does not meet up to these must have standards that you have set, then don't compromise and lower your standards to meet him half way. You both have values that should not be compromise; the key is talking things out completely before rushing into marriage (Nerdlove, 2011).

HAVE FAITH AND TRUST IN EACH OTHER

Faith and trust is paramount to any budding relationships that will inevitably blossom into a permanent thing with rings (no pun intended). It is detrimental that you develop a solid level of trust between you and your partner, after all, how else can you establish a firm relationship (Nerdlove, 2011).

DON'T RUSH INTO MARRIAGE JUST FOR SHOW.

Maintain a level of self-identity and don't allow the person you're with to define you as a person. You are unique special and exquisite in your own special way. Do not allow your sight to become shadowed by the face of your future husband, don't get married just to maintain your status, do so because you truly love the person and wish to spend the rest of your life with him (Nerdlove, 2011).

INDULGE IN SOLITUDE

If you are comfortable with yourself and spending time alone with yourself then you will be better able to share yourself and be of great company to your soul mate (Stutzer & Frey, 2003).

KNOW THE FACTS

Be sure to divulge, dissect and analyse all the known and unknown factors before heading into marriage. Talk about topics such as health status, financial standings, religious backgrounds as well as philosophies. This is critical because now they may sound simple but later they could mean the difference between a happy marriage and a divorce (Nerdlove, 2011).

ARE YOU READY FOR MARRIAGE CONT'D

TRY LIVING WITH A NON-FAMILY MEMBER FIRST

This is a great way to test your habits and attitudes as well as learning what people, other than close family members thinks of you. Consider this as testing the water s before getting married. Do you snore; non-family members will be more honest than family (Stutzer & Frey, 2003).

FOCUS ON ESTABLISHING A CAREER FIRST

This is a bit of a cliché but the sentiments holds true. Working on your career before marriage allows you time to see what you want to become and where want to go before the challenges of a relationship, begins to press on you and distract you from fulfilling your true potential (Stutzer & Frey, 2003).

INVEST TIME IN BEING AROUND KIDS

When you expose yourself to what is entailed in the challenge of raising a child by getting first-hand experience with kids, you will then be able to decide whether are not you want kids when you get married. This can be a deal breaker for a guy who has high expectations where kids are concerned (Stutzer & Frey, 2003).

RESOLVE MAIN REASON FOR GETTING MARRIED

Are you in love with your partner enough to marry him? This is also a cliché but the sentiment is very true, some people get married for many reasons other than love. Some people will get married only because they like the idea of getting married, some just want to wear a wedding gown, exchange rings and have a big fancy after-party. Some people even get married because they feel they are getting old and it is just the natural thing to do at that age. Ascertain your true reasons for getting married before tying the knot (Stutzer & Frey, 2003).

BE FAIR IN EVERYTHING

Challenges in relationships are common everyday situations that only serve to add spice and value to your life after marriage, ensure that when these disagreements occurs, that you be as fear as possible in your dealings. Never rush to conclusions until you have the facts and try to be as equitable as possible in your resolution (Nerdlove, 2011).

ACCEPT PEOPLE AS THEY ARE

People comes in all different shapes, size and characters both internally and externally, don't pressure anyone into changing for you, a marriage among two people means, they both accepts each other's strengths and weaknesses as well as their flaws and imperfections (Arp, 2014).

ARE YOU READY FOR MARRIAGE CONT'D

ASSESS HOW TO DO THINGS YOURSELF

If you are going into a lifelong commitment, ask yourself what you have to offer to the relationship. Can you take care of yourself effectively in the absence of your spouse? Cooking and housekeeping are just two of the many things most men are hopeless at doing for themselves. Ensure that the man you marry is well able to fend on his own before marriage (Nerdlove, 2011).

MEET HIS FRIENDS

Meeting your fiancé's friends will provide you with a wealth of information such as hints and clues in helping you to be sure you chose the right guy and decide whether are not he's suitable marriage material (Nerdlove, 2011).

MEET HIS FAMILY

Meeting your fiancé's family is more than a big deal so doesn't ever think otherwise. These are the people that will be in your life for the rest of your time with him so get to know them completely. Ascertain if there are any hidden family drama and whether or not you are able to deal with such a problem (Nerdlove, 2011).

UNDERSTAND WHO YOU ARE

Understanding yourself should be a no-brainer for many; however, it is not a simple for many women who struggle with personality disorders. Without sufficient knowledge of who you are and is uncomfortable in your own skin then you won't be able to know what type of person you are interested in and willing enough to share the rest of your life with (Stutzer & Frey, 2003).

SINCERITY IN APOLOGY

The clincher her is that we continuously default on our promises and assurance, admittance is showing your partner that you were wrong and also mature enough to make amends and do whatever it takes to make things right in setting the relationship back on its route to success. Without a sincere heart and a mutually apologetic spirit then the relationship will be challenging and met with several obstacles. Understand that when you apologize you don't lose your stand but shows your partner that you are a mature individual. Only mature persons should be engaged in marriages and so if you are too egotistic to say you're sorry then you are too immature to marry (no pun intended) (Nerdlove, 2011).

CHAPTER 14:
Marital Relationship

"The difference between an ordinary marriage and an extraordinary marriage is in giving just a little 'extra' every day, as often as possible, for as long as we both shall live."

—Fawn Weaver

MARITAL PROBLEMS 101

Statistics have shown that 9 out of every 10 marriages in the United States, goes through some form of marital problems within its first year. This substantiate the claim that it is only in the rarest of situations, one finds a couple that is unaccustomed to marital problems. Keeping a proactive mind is critical here where you analyse and identify ahead of time, the nature and technicality of those marital challenges, which when carefully assessed will allow you to resolve them with the least fuss. According to family and marriage therapist Mitch Temple, author of the book The Marriage Turnaround, regardless of the diverse nature of the challenging in marital relationships, successful couples have been able navigate these obstacles and keep their love boat afloat (US Stats, 2013). These couples are longsuffering and enjoy great stick-to-itiveness as they tackle the challenges head-on, whilst learning how to work through the intricacies of their existence. Couples have sought to accomplish this fete by appraising do-it-yourself help books and literatures, participating in conferences, seeking expert assistance, careful studies of physical subjective couples or even through the simple process of success and failure (Stutzer & Frey, 2003).

RELATIONSHIP PROBLEM: COMMUNICATION

Most problematic relationship, are a direct cause of ineffective communication. According to Elaine Fantle Shimberg, author of Blending Families, the cause of relationship disconnect is the breakdown in face-to-face communication where couples try to communicate while talking, texting or chatting on their smartphone, while watching TV or tuning in to your favourite game on your android tablet, " (Stutzer & Frey, 2003).

PROBLEM-SOLVING STRATEGIES:

Be sure to set aside a definite slot from your busy schedule for one on one communing with each other. Shimberg believes, that once you're married and in a full time relationship, and you find that you can't communicate well with all that's happening around you, then you should consider putting your cell phones on vibrate, putting the kids to bed and set the default system to retrieve your calls while engaging in good serious sessions of communing. Consider going out to a public spot, such as a library, mall, recreational park If you can't "communicate" without raising your voices, go to a public spot like the library, park, or restaurant where you'd be embarrassed if anyone saw you screaming. Set up some rules. Try not to interrupt until your partner is through speaking, or ban phrases such as "You always ..." or "You never ...." Use body language to show you're listening. Don't doodle, look at your watch, or pick at your nails. Nod so the other person knows you're getting the message, and rephrase if you need to (Stutzer & Frey, 2003).

RELATIONSHIP PROBLEM: COMMUNICATION CONT'D

For instance, say, "What I hear you saying is that you feel as though you have more chores at home, even though we're both working." If you're right, the other can confirm. If what the other person really meant was, "Hey, you're a slob and you create more work for me by having to pick up after you," he or she can say so, but in a nicer way (Nerdlove, 2011).

RELATIONSHIP PROBLEM: SEX

Even partners who love each other can be a mismatch, sexually. Mary Jo Fay, author of Please Dear, Not Tonight, says a lack of sexual self-awareness and education worsens these problems. But having sex is one of the last things you should give up, Fay says. "Sex," she says, "brings us closer together, releases hormones that help our bodies both physically and mentally, and keeps the chemistry of a healthy couple healthy." (Stutzer & Frey, 2003).

PROBLEM-SOLVING STRATEGIES:

Plan ahead. According to Fay, couples should set appointments and reserve time Plan, plan, plan. Fay suggests making an appointment for sexual pleasures as well as clearing busy schedule just for the sole purpose of love-making. You should be spontaneous she says, and not only schedule time on weekends or during the nights. You could add a bit of spite to your sex-life by pleasuring each other during your lunch break, taking a quick pits stop at home for 30 minutes can really add an element of mystery to an otherwise lethargic relationship (Uprety & Adhikary, 2008). You could do it during the baby's Saturday evening snooze or have a "quickie" in the mornings before work. Create space and time for sex with you and your partner by asking your friends or family to host the kids for a sleepover every other Friday night. Having sex on the forefront of your busy schedule will increase your anticipation for it. Monotonous won't work here, diversifying your sex-life, which will make it into a well anticipated fun-filled encounter. Spontaneous sex venue will blow the chemistry through the roof, have you ever tried having sex in the kitchen? Try doing it in front the fireside or even in the half-way of your home (Stutzer & Frey, 2003).

Explore your sexual fantasies and learn what truly turns you on. Conversely, learn what makes your partner go wild and exploit his pleasure sensors. You can easily do this by crafting a "on and off" list together. This list will tell your partner what you don't like about sex and having sexual relations as well as what gives you erotic salivation when thinking about sex. You will also benefit from knowing what makes your partner tick and what breaks his mood. Note though that not all he likes to do will be to your utmost liking and the reverse of this also holds true. The advice here is to find a point of mutual compromise and try to meet each other halfway (Nerdlove, 2011). Don't be a taker; many women have the notion that it is up to the men to ensure that they themselves are satisfied whilst pleasing her. This is call "amber taking" and is often considered as a mood breaker for the sensual male. Men are emotional creatures even though they sometime hide their true feelings, nevertheless, don't be fooled; they want the same level of attention they give to you during sexual intercourse in return. Be sure to read widely, what sex educational videos or attend sex-ed seminars in a bid to teach you how to give him your full attention, love and support him whilst reciprocating the attention given.   Swap the lists and use them to create more scenarios that turn you both on. Finally, if after trying all these alternatives, you are still unable to resolve your sexual relationship problems, it is recommended that you speak with a sexologist or sex therapist to assist you both in addressing and resolving the issues.

RELATIONSHIP PROBLEM: MONEY

Financial struggle is a world-wide phenomenon which have shackled the advancement of the human race since its conception in the early 10th century. Relationships are not immune to financial challenges and are often the hardest hit in times of economic downturns. The truth is that money challenges may even be prevalent prior to the exchanging of even a single vow. Financial burden is often times attributed to the lavish distribution of monetary tokens for the (self-inflicted), high cost of courting as well as from the high financial requirement of planning for marriage and life after marriage. According to the National Foundation for Credit Counselling (NFCC), couples who constantly find themselves in monetary dilemmas should make time to sit and have a talk either amongst themselves or with a certified financial consultant about their finances (Bettie, 2008). Care should be taken to locate the source of the dilemma as well as what alternative routes to follow in charting a road back to financial success. Financial woes have the tendencies of destroying marriages and driving wedges between families. You may find yourself suffering from high influxes of unpaid bills and mortgages, as well as bankruptcy. The key here is recognizing signs which indicate that you are heading for a negative personal net profit and taking the necessary corrective measures as described below (Washburn & Christensen, 2008).

PROBLEM-SOLVING STRATEGIES:

Honesty is the best policy. Do not hide your financial challenges; provide a true reflection of the pitfall the relationship is in to your partner. Most women likes to feel independent and will attempt to show that by paying the bills and clearing the mortgage, while this is admirable, the true virtue is being cooperative enough to share it with your partner whenever you find yourself in a bind. Nevertheless, take care to approach the situation with the right timing and temperament, if thing are in disarray, then you cannot continue the same lifestyle as you were previously accustomed to, neither can you approach the subject in the heat of the battle. Allow sufficient time to elapse, set aside ample time that is mutually convenient and non-threatening (Washburn & Christensen, 2008). You need to acknowledge that one party may have safer hands with money than the other (he/she can save). One party may be a saver and the other a spender; however, there are benefits to both, thus learn from these trends. Never without critical income or debt from the relationship, attend the discussion with requisite documents. Refrain from pointing fingers, together you must now reconstruct a monthly or annual budget that involved savings, ascertain which party will be responsible for bill payments, whilst allowing free space where both of you have the autonomy to a determined sum to spend at his/her discretion. Determine long term and short term goals whilst making allowances for individual goals with family goal always taking precedence. Include in this discussion an old-age financial package for both party's' parents as well as how to effectively care for them when and should the need arises. Once again, if this proves futile, consult a financial adviser (Nerdlove, 2011).

RELATIONSHIP PROBLEM: FUSSING OVER CHORES

As you grow into a more social and less romantic setting with the arrival of children and the pressures of working a long and hard nine to five whilst taking care of your spiritual emotional and social needs, it can be a real test at time to add household chores in the mix (Stutzer & Frey, 2003). If you are a working woman with kids and household chores to care for and accomplish respectively, then there will be time when you become flustered and retaliate by exchanging a few harsh words to your spouse especially if you feel he has not been assisting you around the home. Most couples are involved in more than one job and may be constantly over extending themselves to make ends meet. Therefore, it is critical that the household chores be divided equitably amongst both spouses, bearing in mind the additional activities each has to accomplish on a daily bases. According to Paulette Kouffman-Sherman, equitable does not necessarily means equally distributed but rather fairly distributed. Care should be taken that one partner is not left to bear the brunt of the household chores while the other sit and talk on the phone with friends or play video games. Work should be fairly and equitably distributed with the acknowledgement of the additional activities to which both party will have to commit to.

PROBLEM-SOLVING STRATEGIES:

The key is to become clear as to what your individual and collective roles in the home are. You must also be ensure that you mutually delegate chores and if necessary, create a timetable to document the activities each spouse is required to accomplish on a daily basis. Be orderly in your job allotment and maintain consistency. Kouffman-Sherman, believes that all jobs should be document to negate the challenge of contention in the home and that both party should be given a chance to accept or reject a chores whilst providing a suitable alternative , the key is to always be fair so that no resentment develops. Always keep a level head and a open mind other solutions or alternative, if are housework avoiders, then maybe you could consider hiring a cleaning agency to do the work for you. If only one partner likes doing housework then the compromise may be that the other partner could considers doing the laundry, mowing the lawn or pruning the garden. Be spontaneous with your efforts, if he likes to cook, do the laundry and clean the house then allowing him the honour of doing so while you try to do other activities such as taking out the garbage or watering the plants. The key is being open minded and a willingness to compromise, switch things up a bit or exchange roles periodically (Washburn & Christensen, 2008).

RELATIONSHIP PROBLEM: RELATIONSHIP NOT A PRIORITY

The biggest pitfall of a true relationship is that we neglect it with the thinking that we are superficial and our partner must allow us to feel as such. The fact is, a relationship is a two way steam that pushes against each other with much alacrity. The truth is that many people enter into marriage with the thinking that they will be loved, appreciated, happy and cherished (Washburn & Christensen, 2008). There is some truth to this, but the problem is that there is no love inside marriage; you are the one who put the love, the joy the excitement, the honour and the respect in marriage. Many people enter into marriage expecting only to receive but not to give. The fact is that it doesn't work like that and even if you are lucky and it works out for you initially, the constant pampering with dry up eventually if you refuse to water and propagate it (Anderson, 2013). To keep your marriage intact, make your relationship the centre of your focus. The hard work does not end when you say "I do" actually, that's where it all begins, Many relationship fail because people fail to make them work. They become comfortable in their current state and stop doing the pleasantries that kept him interested. Overtime, unnourished relationships tend to lose their shine; making you relationship a priority will allow you to rekindle this shine and make it last.

PROBLEM-SOLVING STRATEGIES:

Revamp the things you did in the initial stages of the relationship, make them even more impressive than they were before, consider the things you did on the first date when you first met and try to recreate that first date. Flowers, candlelit dinner under the stars and late night rendezvous by the beachside will spark some heat in your relationship. Consider telling him you love him without words or in some unconventional manner, like baking a cake and decoration it with the words "I Love You". This will certainly strengthen his love and admiration for you (Nerdlove, 2011). Tell him you appreciate him just as he is, compliment him for fixing breakfast or cleaning the house, call, text, skype, IM or tweet him throughout the day, show him that you are madly in love with him. If he hasn't been reciprocating these feelings, it means that he may have gotten married for some other reason than love. They key is to be sure that you are able to live independent lives but just can't keep away from each other. The advice goes further to planning date nights and scheduling time together out of your busy schedule just as you would for any other major event in your life. Mutual respect is the key, continuously say "Thank you," "I'm sorry," "I appreciate you, and I cherish you." Ensure your spouse knows that he means the world to you (Stutzer & Frey, 2003).

RELATIONSHIP PROBLEM: CONFLICT

C onflict is a common factor in all functional relationship, any relationship the exist without any form of conflict whatsoever is not a happy or truthful one and means that one spouse is hiding his/her true emotions for the benefit of the other. This is not a true relationship as all relationship needs conflicts in order to be classified as healthy. Conflict is a part of everyday life and occasionally, you will find yourself involved in some form of dilemma or disagreement with your spouse. This is necessary as not always will you be able to see things eye-to-eye and agree on terms (Anderson, 2013). According to social psychologist Susan Silverman, conflicts are inevitable, however, if you or your partner feels as though you are getting flustered and agitated over the same arguments and the same things keep reoccurring in short intervals, it is cause for concern and a third party's input such as a minister of religion or a family counsellor may be on the cards in short order. When you make a genuine effort to discuss the issue and arrive at an amicable agreement, you may just be on the route of lessening the anger in your relationship and underlying the underlying factors of your issues (Stutzer & Frey, 2003).

PROBLEM-SOLVING STRATEGIES:

Analysing the issues behind the squabble is a safe route to take in resolving the situation but first, you need to find a way to discuss the issues and debate them with your partner without becoming too antagonistic, it is possible to argue in a more civilized and thoughtful manner. You and your partner can learn to argue in a more civil, helpful manner, Silverman says. Adopt these strategies and make them a part of who you are in the relationship. First, understand that you are not a victim in distress, not one is attacking you, the key is to remember that tempers will fly and when they do then the heated words will follow pursuit. It is also your free will to determine whether to respond as well as how you will respond (Stutzer & Frey, 2003). Think logically, are your quarrels characterized by the genuine spirit to resolve the issues or are you more concerned about repaying for past battles that you've lost?

Consider examining the comments you made when you last had a fight with your spouse. Were your comments blameful and hurtful? If yes then you were more interested on payback rather than resolution (Stutzer & Frey, 2003). The next time you engage in a squabble, take a few deep breaths then change your approach. Be spontaneous in your responses, if you're repeatedly involved in retaliating in a certain way which only brought you more hurt and pain then can't expect a different result this time unless you change your strategy. Subtle changes can make a huge difference, if you are impulsive, you may want to consider curbing that and waiting for the appropriate time to but-in. This may be a big help in changing the entire complexion of the conversation. Extending just a small portion of patience and apologizing where necessary is a hard fought test but the result can be extensively rewarding. Since you can't control your partner's behaviour, control yours, and reap the sweet rewards (Stutzer & Frey, 2003).

RELATIONSHIP PROBLEM: TRUST

Having faith and trusting in each other is an integral part of any relationship. To be in the place where you are still having mistrust even after marriage is not an easy issue to handle as trust is the ability to believe that your spouse will love and adore you, put you first, and cares for you whilst being there through thick and thin without any question, comments concerns or remorse (Anderson, 2013). This level of aptitude is extremely difficult to attain and only a few couples are able to reach these heights in their relationships. With trust, you are in a vulnerable place as you now rely on the conscience of your spouse to uphold your indwelling emotions. To all relationships, trust is key; are you privy to certain actions virtues and or inclinations that causes you to not to trust your partner? It may also be that you have unresolved dilemmas in your past that has been hindering your from totally trusting your partner. Key here is the notion that trust is never gained overnight but through a continuous process of growth in love and experience overtime with your partner (Stutzer & Frey, 2003).

PROBLEM-SOLVING STRATEGIES:

- The key to resolving the issue of trust in your relationship is to follow these directives:
- Maintain Consistency in all your doings.
- Promptly show up for all schedule events and dates with your partner
- Say what you will do and do what you say. Action speaks louder than words
- Always maintain the truth in every situation, and withholding of the truth is the same as lying
- Be equitable in you discourses
- Maintain sensitivity to the emotions of others. Agree to disagree, however, never underplay your partner's feelings.
- Maintain accuracy, if you promise to call then call
- Drop in to advice of your late arrival from work
- Absorb and equitable amount of the workload at home
- Remain calm done lose you composure when this goes array
- Think before you talk, never say hurt words you can retract
- Let sleeping dogs lie where they may, never try to rehash hurtful situation
- Make boundaries and keep them
- Jealousy is not always bad but there is a limit you should not exceed
- Listen twice as much as you talk.

RELATIONSHIP PROBLEM: TRUST CONT'D

The facets of a relationship is laced with challenges obstacles and conflicts, however, according to Sherman, several step could and should be taken to minimize marital problems at least, if not avoid them altogether. The call is to consider being realistic at the diverse nature of relationships and how people act in a closely knitted marriage with children. Sherman strongly believes that we should ask for what we want in a relationship directly (Washburn & Christensen, 2008). She further posited that, just assuming your spouse will meet all your heart's desires without you telling him is a silly and futile materialistic thinking that will only bring us further hurt and thus should not be continued. Sherman believes that we should use humour as a medium learning how trivial things slide and enjoy each other for who we really are. In summary, you must be enthused about extending great efforts on your relationship whilst contemplating the way forward. Resist the thinking that life would be a bed of roses if you were involved with someone else; this is far from the truth as everyone has their likes and preferences. The only way to correct marital problems is to address them head-on, the limited knowledge, skill and competences that you have now, will be there in the future to pose greater challenges regardless of the relationship you're in. So take heart and work assiduously to fix your marriage starting with the countless tips provided in this chapter (Stutzer & Frey, 2003).

CHAPTER 15:
Strengthening the Bonds

MAKING STRONG MARRIAGES

"The difference between an ordinary marriage and an extraordinary marriage is in giving just a little 'extra' every day, as often as possible, for as long as we both shall live."

—Fawn Weaver

FLUSHING OUT THE SLUDGE

It is essential for couples living together under a bond of marriage to work assiduously at maintaining and sustaining this bond (Rosenfeld, 2012). It is often very easy to become overwhelmed by our daily routines such as work, house duties, family matters and individual accolades that we forget and sometimes neglect our roles as married couples. The analogy of considering relationship as a flower garden, which we all must tend to, it in a bid to get the prettiest flowers and the healthiest leaves and plants, holds true to as we must excerpt enormous efforts in our relationship if we are to get exceptional results in return. Don't take your relationship for granted, the moment you do will be the beginning of worries and woes in your marriage. If you approach your marital obligations with a lacklustre demeanour, failing to appreciate your spouse for who he is, then the spices and ingredient that assist in keeping your relationship intact will become scarce and you will be heading for trouble (Nerdlove, 2011). Living together after marriage exposes you to your partner's imperfections and shortcoming. Here, you begin crafting verdicts and conclusion about your partner, creating your own beliefs and notions which may be extremely misleading and or irrational. With the realization of these verdicts and beliefs comes the perception that all resulting actions of your partner ultimately relates to your iterated assumption of his immediate character. Here, the hassle is on where there are constant accusations, blame casting, and disparaging of each other (Stutzer & Frey, 2003).

The constant squabble and blame casting is never healthy for any form of relationship as it increasingly distributes a negative atmosphere in the relationship. The ingredients needed for a strong and ever growing relationship are love, passion, intimacy, respect, honesty and trust; once these get shoved behind the rug then you are headed for serious implications. Many couple are inclined to fight each other to the point of separation or even divorce rather than amicably resolving your differences (Nerdlove, 2011). To proof-guard your relationship against such atrocities, it is critical seek additional help from several sources including this book for carefully crafted ideas of preventing catastrophes, resolving differences and improving the intimacy in your relationship. Strengthening the bonds of your relationship requires continuous innovation. Here you must give your best to the cause and refrain from being selfish and dogmatic in your thinking. The true mark of a growing relationship is being able to deal with the challenges as they present themselves in a peaceful and mutually accommodating manner. Think of your partner's points and comments as significant and important. Never downplay an idea regardless of how silly it may seem. You must show your partner that he is worth listening to and sharing with. Once a feeling of inferiority and superiority develops in a relationship then it's safe to say that that relationship is in danger of dying. Once you have a compromising spirit and show your partner how much you love him, then you will be on the path to significantly strengthening your relationship (Nerdlove, 2011).

WHERE IT ALL BEGAN

The natural progression of a relationship stems from the initial dating process then the courting process to the newlyweds status; you've both gone through the planning process for your big day, you've tied the knot with friends, family, loved ones and God as witness, you've legal rights to be together in the form of your marriage license, now what? It is important to know that it doesn't ends here, marriage and family life expert Susan Goth believes that it is critical for us to make a concerted effort to strengthen the core of your marriage and reinforce you newfound commitment in each other whilst caring, protecting it and watching it grow (Washburn & Christensen, 2008). Notwithstanding, it is advised that couples engage in forming their own new and autonomous union together without the infiltration of friends and family members. Sadly, reports have shown that a number of couples have failed to reprioritize the status of their relationship and living arrangements after marriage. There is still a natural bond that exist between the family of each spouse, this bonds may not necessarily need to be severed altogether however, putting parents and siblings first will only had a level of uncertainty to the building of your newly crafted bond. The notion is also true that couples who live alone for an extended period of time before marriage fails to realize that their jobs and friends should no longer be their sole purpose of existence. Accept the fact that you are now in a committed relationship and thus need to acknowledge that your spouse now becomes precedence in your life (Anderson, 2013).

Please note that you still love and respect your parents and you try your best to hang out with friends when you can and attend all family reunions, but in terms of priority, your spouse should be ranked higher than your friends and family. Marriage is your base relationship, all others are flankers, the sooner you establish these boundaries, the easier it will be to hold firm to your partner in later years when things get a bit more complicated. Understand that it may be extremely challenging to make the shift from the mind-set of saying "me" to that of saying "we," no longer can you return to your old apartment (or your childhood bedroom) whenever you become bored, tired and angry or just need some space to think. The excitement of a "girl's night out" or "poker with the boys" no longer forms precedents, here you must take the effects of this on your partner in account before making any hasty decisions. Now you are a team of two and whatever one teammate does has ramifications for the other. According to David Olson from the University of Minnesota in his research on marriage couples, 97 percent of successful and happy couples identified 'togetherness' as a top priority for their success. Engaging in scheduled and unscheduled free time together will definitely boost the status of your relationship. Constantly discussing your activities with your spouse, spending time to offer advice, concerns and comments will go a far way in proving that you truly care about your mate. Happy couples will tell you that their friends and family rarely interfered with their relationship. Ensure that you make your relationship with your partner top priority (US Stats, 2013).

SAFEGAURDING THE BOND

It's essential for you to establish a healthy boundary around your relationship in a bid to safeguard the bonds that have been created by you and your spouse, though this isn't always easy, it's not a rocket science. According to a University of California, Los Angeles interview of 172 newlyweds, factors such as squabbles with in-laws, closeness with friends of the opposite sex and family members have been posited as the main source of the challenges in marriage coupled with communication issues, financial difficulties and mood swings. Marriage is the forming of a completely new family platform, therefore attention should be given to provide care and feeding it with love. Marriage and sex therapist, Pat Love, it is biologically innate in us to be reluctant to give up our space and sense of security all in a single rush, especially if you weren't living together before marriage. Love believes that we are much more comfortable for us to maintain our autonomy and independence when compared to being dependent. The notion is always inclining that you can take care of yourself, without the aid of anyone else. Conversely some Asian cultures are much better at showing us the true meaning of dependency than others. Amae, a Japanese coined anecdote, which when translated means the excited feeling of maintaining interdependency; this is truly a course worth pursuing. Revel in the joy of being exclusive, Love argues. She further states that during the early stages of your marriage, you want to spend some alone time together, just the two of you (US Stats, 2013).

Therefore wrap yourself in the cocoon of exclusivity and guard against any possibility of being disturbed during this time. You may want to consider creating couple rituals by doing a familiar actions together that form a familiar bond that may even serve as a signature of you marriage. You can also spend six minutes to talk before retiring to be for the night. Doing a hand ritual, smiling a certain way, walking a certain way or posing a certain way can be a hidden language only known by you and your spouse heralding a level of romance and passion (Anderson, 2013). Provide daily check-ins terminals where you a mutual medium of communication can be used for checking up on each other. According to Love, couples must engage in a similar policy to that of the large corporations who attempts to keep employees delighted by holding regular conferences. Conversely, the meeting between you and your spouse will be much more appealing than that of a large corporation, hence you will be able to listen and contribute more than what normally happens in larger meetings. The many versions of the daily check-ins, differ from couples to couples, however, all versions should have one main theme which is the effective flow of communication with or without an agenda. Commence your resolution by appreciating a noticeable attribute about each other, while providing new and interesting information about your day if any. Discuss the obvious, inquire of your spouse, the thing that puzzles you the most may it be something about you persona, virtues or attributes (Anderson, 2013).

DISECTING THE ISSUES

Ensure that you season your words with grace when speaking to your spouse, regardless of the mood you are in; it is never tasteful to snap at your partner. Make a concerted effort to control your tempers and replay the thought in your head at least twice before making an utterance. Make a sincere, unwitting complaint-free request that an issue be addressed with utmost urgency ("Honey could you please close the refrigerator for me, it seems you left it opened by mistake and my hands are tied up with making the bed"), conclude your subtle intervention with the notion of hoping ("I hope we can have a romantic dinner tonight just me and you"), you may also want to end with a fair bit of lavish exposition ("I want to spend a weekend get-away in Hawaii on our 10th anniversary"). Before making a major decision, you should ask yourself if it's good for your relationship in the long and short run (Ellison, 2003). If you find that you are in a challenging position where you come up against any important decision that will affect the future of your relationship, consider its impact not just on both parties but on the entire marriage in general. Goth posits that you will be able to know the answer almost instinctively once you give it some careful thought. The clincher here is evaluating how much it will cost you and you partner if you affirm this decision, determine whether things will become too demanding, will involve other individual who may threatens your marriage (dinner with a close ex) or dismal such as separation. Finding yourself in a pickle and being reluctant to ask the question is a demining red flag showing that it's probably not the right time to discuss such matters (Stutzer & Frey, 2003).

Whether it's about the possibility of extended work hours, to buying a new fridge for the home, it's probably not the best thing for your relationship right now. The boundaries you build within your marriage should be healthy ones that will promoted growth and bond building as well. The notion of a semi-permeable membrane holds true for marriages as this allows close family and friends to reach out to you whilst not interfering with the your commitment and goals of your marriage. This can be a bit challenging especially if your immediate family are a bit possessive, however, the key here is deciding each challenge as they come. One such challenge is determining how to deal with holidays. Especially Christmas and thanksgiving, you may want to decide "will I be going to his family's house or my family's house for thanksgiving?" "Maybe we'll just stay in and have a splendid holiday all to ourselves." You may also want to decide how the length of time you'll be spending on the phone with family as well as the extent of marital details that you will disclose to family members. If your husband's family lives in close proximity, decide the frequency of your visits, as well as how often you'll be available to receive visits from them. Most parents, friends and family members will respect your need for privacy and little disturbance, while others may require gentle reminders. Family can make or break marriages says Claudia Arp, life and family therapist at Michigan University. However, you must also note that you marriage can also be a period of transition for them too therefore, don't entirely disconnect from your family, rather, set reasonable boundaries. You need their continued love and support so discuss this with them in the soft and kindest way possible (Nerdlove, 2011).

STRENGTHENING THE BOND

Ensure that you constantly commend your spouse on a job well done according to Claudia Arp. This will be a key ingredient in the mixture of strengthening your marital bonds (Nerdlove, 2011). "Cheer each other on." She says, as one of the most critical things to most men, is knowing that you are there for him and he in return will be there for you, this type of bond is not easily broken. This is simple but straightforward and very important point in a relationship that is often overlooked. Continuous encouragement is a very integral part of the role to play in your relationship Arp posits. She believes that without that continuous encouragement, and then it will eventually be sought from external sources (Nerdlove, 2011). Your partner revels in your encouragement whether the say to you or not. Arp recommends three strategies to combat the challenge of providing critical and thoughtful encouragement. Arp suggests looking for all the positives in your spouse, while developing a sense of humour. Provide honest and specific commendations whilst deciding what you admire about your partner. Arp also suggests that you set time apart for your marriage out of your busy schedule. Make reserving time for your marriage a priority, and refrain from consigning your relationship to leftover time after you have portioned out the rest of your time to other things you classify as significant. When scheduling your time for the next two weeks, start with allotting time for date nights and special dinners for you and your partner first; you may then want to consider adding other activities like spa treatment, mall shopping, as well as gym sessions (Stutzer & Frey, 2003).

You may be so indulged in work and extracurricular activities that you find yourself with little or no time for your relationship, you become absent from the decision making and then it all downhill from here on out. The advice here is for you to consider doing a calendar review, if you find that you are overly swamped with outings with close friends, visits with your family, pressure-filled hobbies, extended time on the job, offering yourself as a volunteer and committing yourself to community development (Anderson, 2013). All these are admirable traits, however, you are not performing you matrimonial role if these activities can be seen as robbing you of quality time to spend with your spouse in spending time just casually chit-chatting, scheduling date nights, as well as delivering on your sexual obligations. This is often overlooked, but if you spend all your evening on the internet watching extended TV series and or marathons then you are also slacking on your role as a spouse. The only strategy for success is giving your relationship a higher priority than that which you share with your close friends and family, without this you won't have a growing relationship. Don't be a workaholic, know when to hit the stop button, disembark from the 27/7 train and unwind with your partner. Exorbitant usage of smartphones and PDAs, Android devices, high-tech pagers and all the other gadgets that maintain our connections with the outside world can both mute the love and intimacy in your relationship and download chaos in your marriage (Stutzer & Frey, 2003).

STRENGTHENING THE BOND CONT'D

A recent study at the University of Wisconsin-Milwaukee discovered that the use of technology usage and moods are positively correlated. According to researchers, couples participated in the transmission and reception of high volumes of calls and messages are more likely to lose track of time and have an influx of work and that goes unaccomplished due to misappropriation of priorities (Washburn & Christensen, 2008). The evasive nature of electronic devices has continued to blur the line between work and play. "This has sought to rob married couples of quality time to spend conversing and strengthening the bonds of their marriage. Be very sure not to fall prey to this marital pitfall as many marriages have gone asunder due to the prevalence of smartphones and other devices. Setting relieve you from impending challenges, consider telling your employer that you cannot take home any work assignments for the weekend as this time as already been apportioned to be spent with your partner. Be sure to tell your human resource department that work related phone calls at home is a no....no. Check all your emails in the evening after work and not periodically throughout the day (Nerdlove, 2011). Incoming calls should only be accepted on the bases of urgency, if a call is not urgent, don't be afraid to say "I'll address the matter as soon as I get to work in the morning." If these calls persist, don't be afraid to turn off all your communication devices at a certain time in the evening letting all callers know that they won't reach you during this time in the evening. Finally, to strengthen the bond, create a code name for love. Maybe you could try using the phrase "olive juice" if you try it together with your partner, then you'll realize your mouth makes the exact movement as when you say the phrase "I Love You." It is critical that you find a secret yet fun-filled expression to publicly display your love for each other that only you know about. This works just fine if you want to maintain your spouse's anonymity while talking on the phone, it with create the "just me and you" feel when used (Stutzer & Frey, 2003).

CHAPTER 16:
Make it Last Forever

"Being in a long marriage is a little bit like that nice cup of coffee every morning – I might have it every day, but I still enjoy it."

— Stephen Gaines

SECRETS TO MAKE YOUR RELATIONSHIP LAST

R oad bumps are there to make us better drivers, the same notion can be applied to relationship ups and downs; they are there to make you into an excellent partner. Most if not all long-term relationship are rocked with terrible road bumps, which often presents themselves at the time when you least expect it. Comprehend the navigation system of your relationship and safely navigate through these road bumps with the least bit of damage to your love life or before you are thwarted into a ditch. Regardless of the duration of time you've spent with your partner, you should know the basic and most simple fundamentals of coursing the road of marriage (Nerdlove, 2011). Though experience teaches wisdom, many couple fail to put what they have learnt into full practice. Though this isn't always easy, it can be achieved through patience and understanding. This is a critical move so take your time while practicing the basic of making it last longer by have fun, having good sex , trusting your partner and showing him affection will make it last forever, but here are a few detail tips on how to make it last (Anderson, 2013).

BE VOCAL ABOUT THINGS YOU LIKE

Keep your conversations fresh and sincere. If you have a liking for something he does or doesn't do then you must be very vocal about this. The effect of everyday dullness, foiling and constant annoyances can drench the catalyst between spouses. Conversely, when the marriage is joyful, spontaneous, refreshing and vivacious, then the flame between you and your partner will be ignited with much alacrity (Arp, 2014). It is recommended that you take the time to make your relationship a reality, this can never be overemphasized. This is where ensure that you give each other your undivided attention when the need arises. It is worth a wealth of sorry and apologies (up to 20) to undo the hurt caused by a negative remark (Nerdlove, 2011). Therefore, it is advised that you provide telling compliments when he helps out around the house or change the pipe fittings even if it still dripping a little. Tell him how beautiful he looks in his new shirt even if you think he should have gotten another colour. Send him a quick voice note, and short message or a brief call to checking and tell him your thinking of him. Ensure these pleasantries are heartfelt and specific, while you smile and make eye contact. If you are able to accomplish everything up to this point, then you will be able to not only turn him on but to make him happy (not only sex). Moreover, these were some of the things you did when you met initially, this will depend your connection emotionally and you'll find that you every time is the right time when it comes to loving him, you'll share hot long kisses before leaving for work and not just the peck on the cheek (Stutzer & Frey, 2003).

TOUCH EACH OTHER

The sense of touch is critical for any relationship to be able to successfully face the test of time. Studies have shown that endorphins (feel good hormones) are released when a couple touch each other whether emotionally or sexually. Therefore, don't be afraid to hold your partner's hands during an early morning stroll; you may also want to rub your hand against his cheeks when you whisper good morning or pull his hair back when he's feeling sad or blue (Anderson, 2013). Recap the touches you share during the early stages of your courting, a light tap on his chest or a nice brush on the thighs. Ever increasing the level of touching between you and your spouse will establish an impenetrable fortress of love and affection. This is critical for later years as many couples whom forms closely knitted relationship can stand to whether the harshest of natural disaster in their relationship, being able to ward against infidelity. We already told you how to build and strengthen the bond between you and your partner, we told you to provide a supportive atmosphere for him, we told you to rally for him whenever possible even if woes lurk in the distant future. The more connected you are as a couple, the stronger your love for each other and the chemistry between you grows. Show these affections through touching and caressing each other every day. You should be able to know what touch is a good one and what is a bad one for different situations (Anderson, 2013).

We also told you to keep marital issues a secret between you and your spouse even when you are being pressured by co-works and close friends to do so. Of course with every agreed statute, there are a few exceptions, therefore, only if there are emergencies, let nothing interrupt you from sharing priceless time with you and your spouse. Lock your doors with a do not disturb sign, turn off your smartphones and concentrate on your spouse and the marriage you share with him (Anderson, 2013). Commit a minimum of at least 30 minutes per day for having a quick chat with your partner about your plans, objectives and aspirations. Here, you're not only cementing your marriage but building and maintaining a beautiful friendship. According to several studies from the Oxford University, crafting a beautiful friendship during marriage will payoff overtime, giving rise to the closely knitted and sensual relationship (Stutzer & Frey, 2003). Always allot sufficient time for intimacy, don't be afraid to log it in your daily planner to be sure. Allow the sense of touch to become a mutual language you both speak. You should be able to communicate a plethora of messages through a set of simple touches. Understand what works for you and use it to your advantage. Soft touches means everything is fine with the kids, mild touches means you want to have sex and rough touches mean that there may be pending dangers. Whatever works for you, decide what codes you want to use and have fun communicating with the sense of touch (Washburn & Christensen, 2008).

STOP BLAMING YOUR PARTNER FOR EVERYTHING THAT'S WRONG

The easiest thing for some women to do is to point the finger at their spouses whenever something goes terribly wrong in their relationship. The fact is that it's very appealing to accuse your partner when things don't turn out the way you planned. The reverse however is not the same as when things goes better that what you'd plan you accept most if not all of the glory (Anderson, 2013). Blaming your partner at first glance is not the best safety net for coverage. It's okay to feel angry, disappointed, bored, confused, betrayed and overly stressed over your relationship at times, but casting the first blame on the other party won't solve the issues.   Here, you are now visualizing your mate as the main hindrance of your relationship logging behind and not improving. This is far from the truth, remember in chapter 15 how talked about relationship being a two way stream? The notion here holds true as well. Attempting to manually speak your partner into changing will only back them into a corner where they become very defensive, whilst seeing you in a negative connotation. The effect here is that the effect is minimal and everything remains the same. The responsivity is still unassured and everyone is left unhappy. Classifying your partner as the guilty party means ignoring that he has been good to you up until now; the clincher her is that you must first examining yourself and try to see where you could have done anything better. It is best to fix your flaws first then seek out the flaws in your partner (Stutzer & Frey, 2003). Here, you both will be left with a better feeling as you both feel appreciated and not chastised.

IMPROVE YOUR RELATIONSHIP BY RELAXING

Relaxation is the world's best medicine, when you relax, your brains opens up and you are able to think clearer that before. The social psychologist always says to the single lady seeking companionship "to attract the best you must be the best," the saying holds true for the long-term relationships as well (Anderson, 2013). You must continuously improve yourself if you want to keep your spouse honest and interested. If you are constantly happy then your relationship will be happy and to gain and maintain happiness, one must learn the art of relaxation. If your relationship is happy it means that there are minimal conflicts between you and your partner (Nerdlove, 2011). Do whatever you need to relax, walk a mile each day, take a yoga class, switch to a decaf diet, hone in on a new hobby or skill; just ensure that at the end of the day, you feel relaxed and recharged. Once you are relaxed then you will be happy, and happy couples stay together longer than unhappy ones. It's quite fascinating to see how you were once in panic mood, searching and examining you drawer for that one sexy piece of lingerie to wear to bed or how to do your hair just to meet your spouse or sleep beside him for the first time. Where is all that passion now? Compared to then, you looked angelic, instead of keeping him honest by keeping up appearances you attend to wearing stain sweat and ratty old T-shirts.   While it's time to relax, you must also take you appearance into account, spruce up year looks for your spouse. Get your hair done, floss and brush those beautiful teeth that sparkle when you smile, put on a fancy robe and show him you are spontaneous.   If you feel good about yourself, it will reflect in your aura and he will also catch the fever. Here, you are more likely to make eye contact, which will improve the flavour of your love (Anderson, 2013). And you know what to do next!

FIGHT FAIR

A relationship without conflict is not a healthy one, however we should be able to resolve conflicts in a rewarding a respectful manner. It normal to have conflicts scattered here and there throughout your relationship; the challenge here is how to effectively handle these conflicts. This can only be accomplished in two words, "fight fair." With an arsenal of effective tools and a positive attitude, conflict can be use as the portal where you learn to even more intimate than you were prior to the conflict. Here you have an opportunity to discuss deep burning issues that may have hindered you from truly expressing your love for your partner, with this thrash out and place on the table, any resolution means that you will now be able to either accept the fact that he can't love you fully or adjust so he can (Anderson, 2013). The chance will present itself for you to be truly loved by your mate as well as accepting and adoring his true and vulnerable personality allowing you to build a true and lasting relationship. You must learn to avoid criticising your mate, engaging in unnecessary confrontation with him as well as becoming a hostile wreck. Researches at UCLA found that relationship which ends in divorce could often be characterized by long and harsh squabbles and one couples was always either under attack or on the defensive. The study further shows that couples who were married for an extended period of time and displayed signs of being happy were better able at controlling conflicts and avoiding loud squabbles and fusses. These couple where good at keeping their conversation from spiralling out of control and abstained from using absolute article like "never" and "always." Point here to note is that in the event of a fight, you must at least attempt to change the issue instils a little humour to chill the flying tempers whilst displaying extra appreciation for your partner. In the event of unresolvable conflicts, cry a truce and cool off for a while.

PICK THE RIGHT TIME TO ARGUE

Ensure that you have your fact straight before starting a budding argument with your spouse, ensure that you are well rested and well fed before starting an argument. The key is not to see arguing as a bad thing, once you are engaged in a debate and both parties has varying contentions then that is an argument. It is very much possible for you to engage in an argument without getting angry (Nerdlove, 2011). This very book you are reading is putting forth a number of arguments to you about relationship issues, yet still we are not upset or fighting each other. Season your words with grace and decide on the best approach to take before initiating the argument. Your tone and tempo are two clear signs to what out for when you want to gage your attitude towards your partner. Ensure that your body language is kept in check and provide passive positive and friendly style of conversations when initiating the argument. It cannot be stressed any further for you to have a full stomach before engaging in a complex argument with your spouse. When you are hungry, you tend to think vainly, hence, ensure that you tommy has relatively good supply of food before commencing the argument in a bit to avoid those nasty, angry and distasteful remarks. Engage in complex argument only when you have the mental psyche to handle such issues. Never attempt to deal with marital challenges if you are not fully focussed and mentally involve, you must also be mentally ready to deal with the challenges as they come. When engaging in marital dispute, it advised that you give it your undivided attention, hence, turn off the TV, your smartphone, your notebooks, and you tablets so he knows it is serious and you also need his full attention. Plan to spend the time and stay the course to have the conflict resolved; you can't rush conflict resolution (Stutzer & Frey, 2003).

LEARN TO LISTEN

Keeping a relationship going for decades is not an easy accomplishment; you must have an eye for detail and an ear for listening. When you are too old to listen properly, it is advised you get and hearing-aid (Nerdlove, 2011). According to Steve Harvey in his book, "Act like a man, think like a woman," listening is the single most powerful tool a couple can possess to keep their marriage intact. To be safe, it is often suggested that we listen twice as much as we speak. Scientist believes that this was why we were conceived with two ears and one mouth so we can listen twice as much as we talk. Quite fitting, a coupled that listens to each other's points before butting in will often make it through the rough patches of their marriage and up to the smooth path to drive steer their hearts of love towards each other. The advice is clear, always show respect by giving your spouse enough time to fully complete his sentences. Do not play the blaming game, refrain from throwing insults, desist from criticising bullying or predicting a bad end to your spouse's story, allow him to finish his thoughts. If you refrain from acting out, you would be saving your partner from living in hell. Whenever you realize that your discussion is getting unpleasant and combative, don't interrupt him from making his point, or try to offer a resolution too soon. When the talks become intense, it means that emotions are involved and these need to be heard (Stutzer & Frey, 2003). You should at this point respond by nodding in approval, rephrase the expressions provided short and mild "um-hum," in a bid to show solidarity for the feelings hosing out behind each word. Often times all your partner need is to be heard and not interrupted. He may even want to feel closer to you and want you to understand he really needs to say out loud to someone (Washburn & Christensen, 2008).

Conclusion

In a world where there are so many hear says and nay says about relationship, it is imperative that you are fully aware of the ins and outs of this very delicate and controversial matter as it relates to your happiness. Now that you are made fully aware of the complications and the facts that surround these life-changing affairs, what will be your next step? Your aim should be to find peace and self-worth in the midst of the on-going chaos that's enfolding around you. By now you would have been made fully informed about the dangers and joys of being single, dating and finally the frame of mind to assume when looking forward getting married and making it last.

As you can see, life is an ongoing cycle that teaches us through many different avenues that in order for us to maintain happiness and healthy relationships with others around us; we must first know the differences and the challenges to expect in a committed relationship and thus to have the courage to choose the path that will lead to cultivating this hemisphere of happiness. Because we are all wonderfully made to choose our own rights to choose, the path that I have chosen may not necessarily be the same path that will help you to reach your peak of contentment. Therefore you must choose the path that is fitted for you, and now the ball is in your court, how will you choose? According to Candace Bushnell, "Man may have discovered fire, but women discovered how to play with it." Learn how to develop that spark on your own so when you meet the man of your dream he will be amazed at your personality.

Bibliography

Anderson, R. T. (2013, March 11). Marriage: What It Is, Why It Matters, and the Consequences of Redefining It. *The Heritage Foundation, #2755*(23), 25-37.

Arp, C. (2014, August 4). 12 Dating Tips That Will Transform Your Love Life. *WOMEN'S HEALTH Magazine, 28*(13), 23-36.

Bettie, C. (2008, March 18). LIVING AS A SINGLE PERSON: MARITAL STATUS, PERFORMANCE AND THE LAW IN LATE MEDIEVAL ENGLAND. *Women's History Review, Vol:17*(3), 327-340.

Ellison, M. A. (2003, September 15). Authoritative Knowledge and Single Women's Unintentional Pregnancies, Abortions, Adoption, and Single Motherhood: Social Stigma and Structural Violence. *Medical Anthropology Quarterly, 17*(3), 205-221.

Epstein, R. (2007, February/March). The Truth about Online Dating. *SCIENTIFIC AMERICAN MIND, Vol: 15*(February/March 2007), 28-35.

FISMAN, R., & IYENGAR, S. S. (2008, November 12). Racial Preferences in Dating. *Review of Economic Studies, 75*(13), 117-132.

Hobbs, A. (2008, March 18). It Doesn't Add Up: myths and measurement problems of births to single women in Blackpool, 1931–1971. *Women History Review , 17*(3), 435-454.

Holden, K., Froide, A., & Hannam, J. (2008, March 18). Winners or Losers? Single Women in History 1000–2000. *Women's History Review, 17*(3), 313-326.

Nerdlove, N. (2011, February 13). *Why You're Not Married.* Retrieved July 25, 2015, from Huff Post Style: The Blog: http://www.huffingtonpost.com/tracy-mcmillan/why-youre-not-married_b_822088.html

Redmond, J. (2008, March 18). 'Sinful Singleness'? Exploring the Discourses on Irish Single Women's Emigration to England, 1922–1948. *Women's History Review, 17*(3), 455-476.

Rosenfeld, M. J. (2012, May 13). *Searching for a Mate: The Rise of the Internet as a Social Intermediary.* (T. N. Foundation, Ed.) Retrieved July 22, 2015, from Stanford Educationals: http://web.stanford.edu/~mrosenfe/Rosenfeld_How_Couples_Meet_Working_Paper.pdf

STRAUS, M. A. (2004, April 12). Prevalence of Violence Against Dating Partners by Male and Female University Students Worldwide. *VIOLENCE AGAINST WOMEN, Vol: 10* (7), 790-811.

Stutzer, A., & Frey, B. S. (2003, June 4). Does marriage make people happy, or do happy people get married? *The Journal of Socio-Economics, 35*(12), 326–347.

A

Uprety, M., & Adhikary, S. (2008, March 21). PERCEPTIONS AND PRACTICES OF SOCIETY TOWARDS SINGLE WOMEN IN THE CONTEXT OF NEPAL. *Occasional Papers, 11*(23), 244-253.

US Stats. (2013, February 28). Marriage and divorce: patterns by gender, race, and educational attainment. *U.S. BUREAU OF LABOR STATISTICS Monthly Labor Review, 173*(1), 1-19.

Washburn, C., & Christensen, D. (2008, November 16). Financial harmony: A key component of successful marriage relationship. *The Forum: For Family & Consumer Issues, 13*(1), 28-37.

www.ingramcontent.com/pod-product-compliance
Lightning Source LLC
LaVergne TN
LVHW051417080426
835508LV00022B/3125